SOMETHING

out of

PLACE

WOMEN AND DISGUST

Eimear McBride

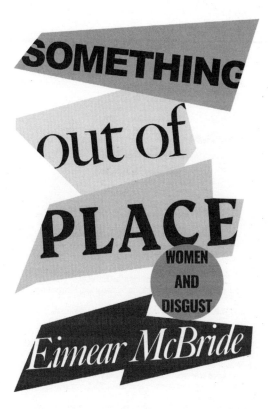

SOMETHING
out of
PLACE

WOMEN AND DISGUST

Eimear McBride

P

PROFILE BOOKS

wellcome collection

Again, for Éadaoin

First published in Great Britain in 2021 by
Profile Books Ltd
29 Cloth Fair
London EC1A 7JQ
www.profilebooks.com

Published in association with Wellcome Collection

**wellcome
collection**

183 Euston Road
London NW1 2BE
www.wellcomecollection.org

1 3 5 7 9 10 8 6 4 2

Typeset in Elena by MacGuru Ltd
Printed and bound in Great Britain by Clays Ltd, Elcograf S.p.A.

A CIP catalogue record for this book is available from the British Library.

ISBN 978 1 78816 286 9
eISBN 978 1 78283 572 1

FSC
www.fsc.org
MIX
Paper from
responsible sources
FSC® C018072

FOR STARTERS

As I type the female population of the world stands at 3,859,840,727, making women about 49.6% of the global population and meaning there are a lot of us around. Everyone knows a woman or has at the very least been brought into the world by one. We're always there as well, in the shops, down the pub. We can often be seen on hospital wards, public transport, in sports arenas or on the telly. You will find us both working and shopping at Asda. Some of us are astrophysicists. Some of us run dry-cleaning businesses. We are engineers and teachers, local councillors and orthodontists. We can frequently be found in our homes shouting at our children or on the other end of a call centre line, being shouted at. Sometimes we are even responsible for feeding time at the zoo. The truth of the matter is that women are pretty much everywhere, doing all kinds of stuff, all the time.

Given our louring omnipresence then, what might be the origin of all this disgust that's so continually directed towards us? By 'disgust' I mean the disgust that appears to mystically attach itself to the female body at birth – although sometimes too upon the mere determination of sex in the womb – and then proceeds to pursue that body right through each stage of its being, especially the later ones though, it should be said.

How has this disgust managed to settle itself in as a kind of default reaction to almost every aspect of women's lives – being some-times rampant and ill-concealed, while at others, insidious and almost imperceptible?

Certainly, it performs its abhorrence so diligently – enthusiastically even – that a constant alertness to disgust's objections and proposed limitations has become one of the great, inexorable presences in those lives. It's there in the proprietorial, fetishistic attitudes towards how we look, what we weigh and what we wear, to the ways we think about the world, how our bodies experience the world or are forced to experience the world. Sometimes the disgust is expressed broadly and unthinkingly. Sometimes viciously and particularly. Economically and politically. Culturally and religiously. But always damagingly, and consequentially. As women contain within our vast numbers as much variety of race and sexuality, size and shape, physical ability and disability, intellectual capacity and stupidity, wellness and illness, talents and deficits as the male population, what possible excuse can there be for our being held to this additional standard of 'not arousing disgust'? A problem further complicated by the fact that, radical surgery aside, our bodies cannot but be what they are and do what they do. And, although we have neither say in the constituent parts of this standard nor right of veto over it, we will most certainly bear the brunt of any failure to attain it.

And I'm tired of this, bored by it and constantly infuriated by the barefaced presumption of it. What follows here are my thoughts on the possible origins of this intangible, yet undeniable, disgust, what purposes its evolution might serve and who its beneficiaries must be.

But one more thing before setting out, if sometimes I write as if women all come from the same place and time, or have the same concerns and the same prohibitions placed upon them, this is only a shorthand for noting areas of shared difficulty rather than an assertion of uniformity. I know we are not all the same and that, even though we are sometimes treated as such, women do not run as a herd. One size does not fit all, any more than one history speaks for all or one experience represents all. This is simply an essay, a collection of thoughts, not an objective work of academic research, and so, by its very nature, subjective. Where there are gaps in nuance and knowledge, I hope others will fill them in and push the parameters of the debate further. I do not doubt there is more than enough disgust to go round. This is just my shift, my turn to contribute to an argument that stretches back and forward as far as the eye can see.

DISGUST AND TABOO

First then to the thorny matter of disgust itself. What is it and how do we experience it? It certainly bears a close resemblance to repulsion in its intense distaste for and aversion to specific objects or people. However, where repulsion still allows us – albeit unwillingly – to tolerate the repulsive object, disgust does not. This may be because disgust's roots lie in a more visceral, animal instinct to avoid contact with that which we suspect to be physically harmful to us.

One of humankind's earliest assertions of self is the refusal to put certain foods in our mouths. While, in reality, these foods are unlikely to be detrimental to our health, our personal disgust monitor registers something unacceptable in their appearance, odour or texture which forces us to reject them. As anyone who has ever been charged with feeding a young child knows, once their sense of disgust has been aroused the difficulty of levering in a forkful of broccoli or scrambled egg, or whatever foodstuff has offended, between those unwilling jaws becomes close to insurmountable.

Rachel Herz, the author of *That's Disgusting: Unravelling the Mysteries of Repulsion*, has described this physical disgust as 'a scientific amalgamation of terror management, and avoidance of pathogens and oral incorporation', which seems to accurately capture the sense of dread and urgent need for escape which any disgust reaction immediately provokes. Taking this a step further, in his aptly titled *The Anatomy of Disgust*, William Ian Miller expands on the reach of disgust, suggesting:

> things or deeds we find disgusting put us in the world of disgust when we have

the sense that we would not be surprised should we start feeling queasy or nauseated, whether or not we actually do so. Disgust surely has a feel to it; that feel, however, is not so much of nausea as of the uneasiness, the panic, of varying intensity, that attends the awareness of being defiled.

Miller's idea of disgust as a harbinger of defilement is perhaps closest to the congenital disgust for women and their bodies that interests me, in that it neatly illuminates some of the irrational behaviours exhibited by misogynists in both public and private forums.

But, if this is indeed the case, what is it about women that prompts such feelings of defilement? Feelings strong enough to, apparently, justify male intervention and corrective treatment for what is, after all, the business of women's own lives and bodies? Are we ourselves an unwitting trigger with our, oh-so-modern, insistence that menstruation, possession of the equipment for pregnancy and birth, and the having of a vagina rather than a penis are not in themselves acceptable reasons for dismissing us wholesale from the centres of power? Or is our continual belittlement into the sum of our unavoidable physical characteristics, and biological functions, just a conveniently insidious form of backlash – easily invoked, inclusive of every woman on the planet, devastating in effect and impossible to refute? In many ways it's a clever ploy because in order to provoke disgust in others, logic insists that women must indeed be essentially disgusting.

Perhaps it would help to look at something else which is both naturally occurring and a dependable trigger of disgust? What about dirt then? It certainly carries with it the same concept of defilement and provokes a similar instinct to avoid. No one wants to hear dirt's side of the story and, as for having to suffer an unwelcome presence in every area of your life, well, what could be more disgusting than dirt? Women being treated like dirt is hardly an alien concept either. In *Purity and Danger: An Analysis of Concepts of Pollution and Taboo*, British anthropologist Mary Douglas states: 'If we can abstract pathogenicity and hygiene from our notion of dirt, we are left with the old definition of dirt as matter out of place.' A slice of cake on a plate is not dirt. A slice of cake on the toilet floor, is. The essential nature of the cake remains cakelike wherever it is; the change in its status is caused by our reaction to its placement.

In later editions, Douglas attributed the phrase 'matter out of place' to the etiquette-fixated eighteenth-century statesman Lord Chesterfield – although it was also a phrase widely used in nineteenth-century debates about the growth of cities. While neither the phrase's ostensible originators nor Douglas herself were writing about women or feminism, there is relevance in Douglas's interest in why specific taboos – taboo being the natural ally and logical correlative of disgust – come into force at certain times in certain societies and can, just as quickly, be consigned to the dustbin of history. Take this paragraph then from Douglas's preface to the 2002 edition of the book:

> The study of taboo impinges inevitably upon the philosophy of belief. The taboo-maintained rules will be as repressive as the leading members of the society want them to be. If the makers of opinion want to prevent freemen from marrying slaves, or want to maintain a complex chain of inter-generational dynastic marriages, or they want to extort crushing levies – whether for the maintenance of the clergy or for the lavish ceremonials of royalty – the taboo system that supports their wishes will endure. Criticism will be suppressed, whole areas of life become unspeakable and, in consequence, unthinkable. But when the controllers of opinion want a different way of life, the taboos will lose credibility and their

selected view of the universe will be revised.

Although the term taboo itself only dates back to the 1770s, the idea of the intransgressible social, cultural or religious prohibition has always been with us and remains fully active today. The fanciful assumption in many, post-Cold War, Western democracies that all the old social, racial and sexual taboos had gone the way of the dodo, and that the widespread imposition of taboos had become an obsolete method of communal control, has been given a short, sharp shock in recent years. One need cast only a cursory eye over Twitter to be assured that those who attract the attention of our continuously evolving, contemporary system of taboo, whether by accident or design, are probably more keenly aware than ever of the consequence of falling foul of its evangelical enforcers. Gleeful cancelling, no-platforming, dog-piling, doxxing and the pursuit of individuals beyond the confines of social media into their physical and professional lives are just a few of the outcomes that await those guilty of expressing any but the most non-committal opinions or positions. As women are by far the most regularly targeted group on all platforms, across all subjects and on either side of whichever argument is raging, it's hard not to draw the conclusion that this is contemporary patriarchy exerting its considerable influence over the instigation of new taboos in order to dish out behavioural correctives to women in a highly visible and public manner. The urgency and increasing vehemence with which these taboos are being devised and disseminated can surely be read as a bare-faced backlash against the seismic shift in women's fortunes over the last century or so.

LUCKY BITCHES!

Nowadays, the parameters of our lives are no longer necessarily bounded by the social and familial expectations we were once unquestioningly reared to fulfil, as though the epitaphs for our gravestones had already been carved at birth. The momentousness of closing that distance, between our enslaved or ensnared historical selves and the unbounded futures we wanted to make possible for ourselves and our daughters, was seminal and means we can never again reassume those old roles in a credulous, uninformed state. In truth, we have been changed in a fundamental way and have travelled too far to go back. But, although that Rubicon has crossed, we must remain on our guard against the forces which would really much prefer to make us turn around and march all the way back into our sculleries again.

A hundred years of hard-won, and still inadequately realised, liberation then is a short time indeed when compared to the millennia of female oppression we drag behind and what we have gained is still so new, and so fragile, it must be rigorously protected from the incessant assaults levelled at it by an innately misogynistic system. Witness the self-satisfied line of men photographed with US President Donald Trump as he signed an executive order to ban funding of international groups who perform or provide information about abortion. To these powerful men, today's noisily enfranchised women are never less than a permanent source of aggravation, because the battles they have won have changed the very fabric of the lives those men can now legally lead. Gone are the days of blanket unaccountability for their actions towards women in the workplace and their unquestioned supremacy in the home. As dispiriting as the failure of Donald Trump's 'Grab 'em by the pussy' tape to exclude him from the presidency was, that so many thought it might, and should, was indicative of a huge cultural shift from the days in which it would have been unthinkable for John F. Kennedy's sexual misdeeds to be aired in public by the press. Women's toppling of the traditional male 'masters of the universe' narratives of yore brought not only change for themselves but for all concerned, whether it was welcome or not. After all, Harvey Weinstein bestrode the entertainment industry like a colossus until some brave women put their small, seemingly insignificant, selves in his way and a generation was galvanised as a result. Basic reason suggests those who have been cast out from that consequence-less Eden are unlikely to be grateful for the forced recalibration of their entitlements. It is surely even to be expected that they would not give such privileges up without a fight or easily forgive those who have inflicted this injurious repositioning upon them. And, in an environment in which all-out aggression can no longer be publicly utilised as the first line of defence, might the imposition of taboo provide a promising point of departure for the backlash? Taboo certainly shifts the argument from the what to the who and, as such, makes it all the harder to refute in a collective, definitive way. Mary Douglas says, 'A polluting person is someone who has crossed some line which should not have been crossed and this displacement unleashes danger for someone,' which seems about right.

So, having crossed the line, indeed having changed the very lie of the line, women have unleashed danger for those who cannot, or will not, accept that change. I imagine it comforts these pillars of the old world to think of women as 'matter out of place' and treat us with all the disgust that they feel we are now, by their logic, due.

Which brings us back to dirt. To be seen as dirt or treated as dirt is shaming and the reason shame works so well as a weapon is that, as the Catholic Church discovered centuries ago, its ability to work on the individual has a far greater reach, and impact, than direct authoritarianism can manage. Unlike guilt, which relies on an individual recognising and regretting their transgression, shame operates from the inside. Shame comes about when the individual has cause to regret not only what they have done but who they, fundamentally, are. To feel shame suggests becoming conscious of an innate flaw, an inappropriate, unacceptable element of the self, which cannot be simply apologised for and moved on from. It must be concealed and denied at all costs and, because of this, shame becomes the weapon within. Its nature is self-perpetuating and inescapable and its effects as devastating as they are invisible to the external eye. Ask any victim of sexual abuse what difficulties they encounter after the initial physical trauma is over and you will be left in no doubt about the catastrophic consequences shame can inflict on a life.

Shame has for so long been the default setting for women, instilled early on, drunk in with the metaphorical mother's milk of our society, that it is often hard to differentiate where shame and an authentic sense of self begin and end. But we have, at least, embarked upon the journey of disentanglement now and are, therefore, travelling farther down along it all the time. Perhaps one day we may even arrive at a place in which a blanket refusal to own the stain that shame suggests we possess becomes the natural default, clicking into action from the very outset of life? In order for that to be achieved, however, it's crucial that the sources and sites of that shame are identified. While this is no straightforward task, there is little ambiguity about the place of its first manifestation: the body and, specifically, the body of the girl.

This is where the valuelessness innate to objects of disgust is first grafted on to the lives of women, when they are still children and wholly reliant on the adult world to tell them what they are or can aspire to be. A few years ago, when my daughter was still young enough to watch the children's TV show *Paw Patrol* – in which a group of six dogs run around doing helpful things – I remember her earnestly asking why only one of the dogs was a girl. She also asked why the girl dog had to wear pink but that's for another essay. In that moment, though,

I suddenly recalled all the films and TV I'd watched as child in which girls were either entirely absent or hanging around at the back waiting to scream at spiders, require urgent assistance or kindly nurse someone back to health. I thought of the characters from the classic children's books I'd read, the *What Katy's Dids* and *Secret Gardens* in which nasty, wilful little girls had to be taught to smile and make nice, or the *Pollyannas* clearly driven demented by their inane desire to please. And, to be honest, I was raging. I mean, they're only dogs, why couldn't it be half and half so all the little girls watching could have a choice about which one they wanted to identify with? But this unwillingness to be inconvenienced into catering for the swashbuckling imaginations of little girls is only a symptom of a deeper and darker dislike.

Far more sinister are the estimated 100,000 sex-based abortions performed yearly in India and the 100 million 'Missing Women' of the Nobel-Prize-winning economist

Amartya Sen's 1990 study of the male-heavy population imbalance, believed to be the result of son-preference abortions and the infanticide of female children, as well as insufficient health care and nutritional provision for girls and women. These bleak truths are indicative of the inferior status automatically conferred upon women from the very first disclosure of their biological make-up. So, what part has disgust played in making XX chromosome-carrying foetuses 'out of place' in the womb? Arguments bandy back and forth about the prohibitive economic consequences of rearing girl children in certain cultures, but the case for encouraging an evolution in traditional expectations of the roles women and girls could play in contributing to the economic welfare of those societies, is rarely made. Instead there seems to be an imperturbable degree of content with the status quo. To be so unquestionably expendable therefore, the female foetus must be viewed as innately worthless, or potentially destructive, as well as possessing less true humanity – or the potential for it – than a male foetus. From this position it's a short step to consigning it to the traditional status conferred upon women's bodies everywhere: not that of the simple, physical manifestation of their humanity but an object of unpardonable inconvenience, comprised of just so much meat.

MEAT OR FLESH?

In the 'Speculative Finale' to her 1978 book about the merits and relevance – or otherwise – of the works of the Marquis de Sade, *The Sadeian Woman and the Ideology of Pornography*, Angela Carter examined in some detail the difference between the words 'meat' and 'flesh' when seen from the viewpoint of the pornographer. Writing from, what now seems to us, a more decorous era, less than twenty years after Penguin had fought the good fight over the censorship of *Lady Chatterley's Lover* and with the

World Wide Web still an itch in the paternal pants, Carter could not have foreseen how increasingly resonant her breakdown of the difference would become, and not only as a means of dividing the arty sheep from the dirty goats. Nowadays, it functions as a gauge for separating out genuine efforts to look at, or think about, the female body – most especially the sexual female body – from the perennially modish, often transparently commercialised, objectifications enacted against it. Given how blurred the boundary has become between what we define as meat and what we define as flesh, here are the dictionary definitions:

MEAT
noun
1. the flesh of an animal, typically a mammal or bird, as food (the flesh of domestic fowls is sometimes distinguished as *poultry*).
'pieces of meat'
SYNONYMS: flesh, muscle

2. ARCHAIC: food of any kind.
synonyms: food, nourishment,
provisions, rations, fare, foodstuff(s),
nutriment, daily bread, feed; INFORMAL:
grub, eats, chow, nosh, scoff; FORMAL:
comestibles, provender; ARCHAIC: victuals,
viands, commons; RARE: aliment
'meat and drink'

At its most straightforward, then, it is clear that meat describes the bodies of animals which we traditionally expect to be consumed. Although the word 'flesh' is mentioned as a synonym, it connects – in this definition at any rate – with the meat of poultry, or birds ... the slangy connotations of which, given the context, do seem to require a quick tip of the hat – so, 'tip'. But with that dealt with, here is the same dictionary's definition of flesh.

FLESH
noun
1. the soft substance consisting of

muscle and fat that is found between the skin and bones of a human or an animal.

'she grabbed Anna's arm, her fingers sinking into the flesh'

SYNONYMS: muscle, tissue, muscle tissue, meat, brawn; INFORMAL: beef

'you're as thin as a rake – you need a sight more flesh on your bones'

verb

1. put weight on.

'he had fleshed out to a solid 220 pounds'

SYNONYMS: put on weight, gain weight, get heavier, grow fat/fatter, fatten up, get fat, fill out, thicken, widen, broaden, expand, spread out

'the once lean physique had fleshed out'

2. stimulate (a hound or hawk) to hunt by feeding it a piece of flesh from a recently killed animal.

'I have fleshed my bloodhound'

On the surface, these definitions don't appear to be wildly dissimilar. Flesh even appears in the initial definition of meat, 'flesh of an animal' etc. However, meat does not return the favour and only makes its appearance in the definition of flesh among its more extenuating synonyms. It is safe to say then that while meat and flesh are close in meaning, they are not precise counter- parts. Meat is instantly linked to animals and specifically to food – for, catastrophic cir- cumstances aside, who is dietarily inclined to think of their pet gerbil as 'meat'? – while flesh, on its very first appearance, is con- nected to the human body, with the animal body included only in a secondary role and not particularly regarded as a comestible.

Beyond dictionary definitions then, the lines we draw between the two is evident throughout Western culture. In the Gospel According to St John, Christ advises his followers that whosoever eats of his 'flesh' – rather than 'meat' – will gain eternal life. In Shakespeare's *The Merchant of Venice*, Shylock's demand for his 'pound of flesh' is shocking because the flesh in question belongs to the all-too-evidently human Antonio rather than some unfortunate bullock or ewe. Likewise, Hamlet calls for his 'too, too solid flesh' rather than his too, too solid meat to be dissolved into air. The phrase 'flesh and blood' describes the state of being human – I'm only flesh and blood! – with all its attendant frailties as well as defining a familial relationship – she's my flesh and blood. The Smiths song 'Meat is Murder' was apparently an attempt to persuade people of the moral vagrancy of the carnivorous lifestyle. However, given how mercifully few people ever directly experience murder while every single human being knows intimately what it is to both delight in, and endure, the life of the 'flesh,' it is possible that 'Meat is Flesh' might have proved a more revulsive, if less satisfyingly alliterative, deterrent. Writers frequently use the term 'flesh out' to describe adding depth and humanity to a character. Of course, 'flesh out' can be used in non-human-specific contexts too; to 'flesh out' details of an argument etc. That 'to meatify' is never similarly applied suggests 'flesh' possesses an active mind at work while to 'meatify' is merely an instinctive gain of animal bulk.

So, if the similarities in meaning and usage between meat and flesh are clear, the disparities are as well. Meat and flesh are the same and yet not the same. This may sound like nothing more than a linguistic parlour trick but the fact remains that when their usages are interchanged it is rarely accidental. We notice immediately and understand what is being hinted at. For example, when, in Jerry Seinfeld's animated children's film *Bee Movie*, a cow wails to her lawyer that she feels 'like a piece of meat', we know exactly what the joke is. For children, the reference is straightforward and without the sexual connotation we would immediately infer were the line to be uttered by a woman in a film for grown-ups. Every adult viewing it, though, will be aware of the compound nature of the gag.

The next question must surely be then:

how has it become so passé for the bodies of half of the world's population to be born, reared into adulthood, live, work, reproduce, age and die under the assumption that while they may know themselves to be flesh, they may just as easily find themselves condemned to be viewed, and treated, only as meat?

And how is it that, in the overwhelming majority of instances, this interchange comes to pass without meeting any serious challenge and frequently without being remarked upon at all?

'RIP HER TO SHREDS'

Being a child of the eighties, this thought reminded me of the following story about Debbie Harry which, while now from a bygone era, seems as relevant in this era of negative social media commentary as it was horrible back then.

In 1979 the New York rock band Blondie were at the height of their international chart success, with No. 1 singles and albums in both the US and UK, while their frontwoman, the aforementioned Debbie Harry, was one of the most readily recognisable women on the planet. In that same year Blondie became the subject of a so-called 'fan bio' book by rock music writer Lester Bangs – whose memory and back catalogue of gonzo-style articles are now revered and much-fetishised by fans of New York's music scene at that time. In this 'fan bio' Bangs fills eighty-five or so pages with repeated disparaging references to Harry's age and the fact that she is older than other performers popular at the time – all while constantly referring to her as a 'girl'. He also, with notable consistency, includes the assessments made of her physical appearance by his other interviewees, and very obviously neglects to do the same to the male band members. To top this off, he then goes to some pains to describe what the true effect of her image probably is and suggests that she is either too stupid or too cynical to understand the very real disgust she arouses in men. So, take it away, Lester Bangs:

> I think if most guys in America could somehow get their fave-rave poster girl in bed and have total license to do whatever they wanted with this legendary body for one afternoon, at least 75% of the guys in the country would elect to beat her up. She may be up there all high and mighty on TV, but everybody knows that underneath all that fashion plating she's just a piece of meat like the rest of them.

Even taking into account the antagonistic posturing and inflated chauvinism traditional to the gonzo journalist, it remains disturbingly significant that Bangs felt so comfortable, and vindicated, about launching such a personal, highly sexualised invective against Harry, and then – in case any of us were left in doubt as to the legitimacy of his claim – substantiated it by widening its perimeters to include all women, 'the rest of them'. Presumably rows of enthusiastically nodding male heads was the response he expected to his somewhat slippery attack – slippery in that, while obviously aiming the blow at none but his own behest, Bangs still utilises the hoary old pretence of merely operating as a mouthpiece for the average, unreconstructed American male. In pointing this out, however, I am obliged to admit that because the book then found its way across an editor's desk and into print unhindered, he was entirely correct in his expectation. After all, Debbie Harry was out there for all to see, being 'high and mighty' (successful and uncompromising?) and significantly 'on TV' where, apparently, Bangs felt she – and such qualities in women, generally – had no right to be represented. No outcry, that I can identify, followed the book's publication. In fact, nothing did, except that the quote continues to exist out in the world and Debbie Harry is still to this day asked about how it felt to have been the target of such a personally demeaning insult, particularly as it was hurled by a man who she – and this is even more depressing –once regarded as a friend. As with so many women before and since, Harry, bruised but unbeaten by her public meatification, simply got on with achieving further chart success and Blondie's eventual induction into the Rock and Roll Hall of Fame. Along the way of course she was obliged to endure many further rancorous media carpings about her appearance and age, the like of which is rarely, if ever, aimed at male artists of similar status. Having died of a drug overdose in the early eighties, Bangs has never been asked to account for his peculiarly incontinent bitchiness. Instead he was instantly elevated to the hallowed halls of the 'gutter poet' and 'visionary rock journalist' and has remained there ever since, so ... same ole same ole, I suppose.

Naturally, this is only one example of the tradition of considering women's physical selves as though they are somehow divisible from their thoughts, feelings and equivalent entitlement to be treated like sentient human beings as their opposite numbers over there in manhood. The logical dissonance of this attitude has become so intrinsic to our culture, and therefore to the way girls are reared into women, that it is virtually impossible to unpick its myriad deceptions from the fabric of everyday life. After all, online, on TV, in glossy magazines and everywhere in the media, women are constantly sold clothes, beauty products and the promise of impossible age-eroding miracles which are modelled by girls too young to be accurate representations of the benefits of whatever the cure-all in question is, or else by older women whose true physical appearances have been airbrushed to within an inch of detectable humanity.

The cynicism of this well-worn corporate strategy, of creating anxiety about an apparently unignorable problem while simultaneously advertising its solution, is absolutely reliant on creating a hostile environment for women right at the very centre of their lives, a place of self-disgust, recrimination and inadequacy. This has for the main part been achieved through waging perpetual war on women's efforts to form contented, liveable relationships with their own bodies.

The long-established response to protests about this encroachment tends to follow along the lines of 'no one's forcing women to buy into the highly restrictive beauty culture which just happens to form the exo-skeleton to most aspects of their everyday lives'. This not only bats away calls for change but shifts responsibility for the prevailing atmosphere of commercialised coercion back onto women themselves. It is a method which has proved effective enough to make public confession of crimes against physical perfection become so normalised an aspect of women's lives that even the film stars and models, who provide the 'gold standard' which every other woman necessarily fails to reach, are themselves regularly obliged by the media to admit to everything from their 'least favourite' parts of their bodies to crippling physical insecurities and eating disorders resulting from chronic body dysmorphia.

It seems that whenever the media deems a woman's body to be an isolatable entity, deserving of attention and treatment distinct to the physical and psychological integration customarily accorded to men, a blurring of the boundaries between meat and flesh is never far behind.

TO MEAT OR NOT TO MEAT, THAT IS THE QUESTION

As we have seen then, to make what is flesh into meat – whether for comedic or more sinister purposes – can usually be read as a deliberate challenge to the humanity of the flesh in question and is readily recognisable as such. Given the lengths humanity has gone to over the course of its relatively brief history to mark itself out as separate from, and loftier than, the rest of nature, returning a person to the taboo state of animality is probably one of our more instinctive, if not wittier, insults. Again, former US president Donald Trump's tortuous efforts to demean women who have opposed or questioned him, or who just happened to be in his eyeline when a fit of pique hit, by indulging in pre-teen jibes like 'pig' and 'dog' and 'horseface' is ample evidence of the perceived power of the animal insult – although it's worth noting that, as with schoolchildren, they also seem to be the type of insult instinctively grasped for when coherent argument lies beyond the capability of the name-caller. Certainly, since the advent of Darwin's theory of evolution, the suggestion that women, people of colour and LGBT communities are further down the evolutionary ladder than white, straight males has been a useful device, wielded even by those who refuse to accept that the scientific evidence for evolution outweighs their belief in biblical creationism. That said, the idea that certain humans possess an innate superiority, entitling them to special treatments and dispensations from the legal, financial and moral injunctions placed upon their inferiors, dates right back to the very earliest arrangements of family, community and society. Although the constitutive elements of the superiority and inferiority in question may vary, these still appear to remain the true weights by which the majority of human interactions come to be measured, be they on the personal or global scale. How this struggle for status works within the context of what is meat and what is flesh, then, is a complex one. In *The Sadeian Woman*, Carter quotes de Sade's dictum that: 'The strong abuse, exploit and meatify the weak. They must and will devour their natural prey. The primal condition of man cannot be modified in any way: it is eat or be eaten.'

Despite the banality of the phrase 'eat or be eaten', it remains as popular an excuse as it has ever been among those keen to wash their hands of personal responsibility for any number of illegal and unethical behaviours. However, once read again in conjunction with the first part of the quote – 'The strong abuse, exploit and meatify the weak' – it provides more interesting, if more convoluted, food for thought – may the pun be pardoned. For if this is indeed an accurate representation of the traditional 'dominant male/passive female' dynamic, then while the meatified face the unenviable prospect of being chewed down to gristle, the meatifier must surely bear a more socially ignominious title. Not that of farmer, the one with responsibility for tending the cattle; or even butcher, the one responsible for killing and carving them up; but instead that of cannibal, the one who will eat their own.

AND THE WORD WAS MADE FLESH

While the anthropological world's study of cannibalism remains divided over the causes, meanings and even the factual existence of cannibalistic cultures, there are a few recurrent taboos which have become attached to the theoretical understanding of its functions. The most generally accepted is that cannibalism was a masculine, cere-monial privilege grounded in the belief that, by consuming their flesh, warriors could mystically absorb the strength of their defeated enemies into themselves. Another was that cannibalism was a practice barred to women and, should this rule happen to be transgressed, the males of the society could expect nothing less than a total rever-sal of their fortunes in war ... Coming at the subject from a different angle in her 1994 Reith Lecture series, *Managing Monsters*, the novelist, critic and cultural historian Marina Warner dedicated the fifth of her six lectures, 'Cannibal Tales: The Hunger for Conquest', to the cultural figure of the can-nibal. In referencing acts of cannibalism as represented in myth – Cronus, Zeus, etc. – Warner pointed to the foundational horror upon which the concept of cannibalism rests: 'cannibals fail to see their prey as their kind and this is an act which effectively exiles them from humanity.'

If this is indeed the case, the now metaphorical 'cannibal' falls rather neatly in step with attitudes of the so-called 'alpha male' persona that the patriarchy has pressured and encouraged men to aspire to. In terms of social and sexual status, the 'alpha male' sits at the top of a ladder which no woman can ever hope to climb. He celebrates, and is celebrated for, taking what he wants – when he wants it – and is both willing and able to crush those occupying the rungs below, should they prove to hamper the pursuit of his goals. From Napoleon to Byron, Stanley Kowalski to James Bond, history and culture are littered with envious, salutary accounts of red-blooded males who have vanquished their enemies with either pen or sword – preferably sword – and then drained every ounce of 'their' accompanying woman's energy and attention before casting her aside to move on to the next willing, if unwitting, victim.

The twentieth- and twenty-first-century entertainment industry's fetishisation of the hypnotic, irresistible and all-powerful male vampire might be another example, as is the infatuation with superhuman sportsmen, the romanticisation of violent criminals – the vast majority of whom are male – and the continuous celebration of an explicitly anti-feminist 'lad culture' in the popular media, which is dedicated to slavering over sexual imagery of women while mocking women who do not meet their 'standards' and expressing disgust generally for the physical realities of women's bodies and their accompanying biological functions. In short, we are encircled by florid examples of the level of popular acceptability, not to mention downright hero worship, with which the 'alpha male' is surrounded. Whether in fiction or fact, these figures have always been feted for their unrestrained conquering and/or consumption of others. The 'alpha male', while now a more controversial figure than he once was, remains a potent symbol of the establishment view of the dominant male as a breed apart, one who is held to a different standard and even that being a standard mostly of his own choosing. But then, given the cultural centrality of the figure of the alpha male, perhaps it would be more accurate to say that, in fact, it is everyone else who is a breed apart from him. If this is so, then it begs the question: does the notion of 'cannibalism' really have the power to shock us any more, never mind bring any true social ignominy along in its wake? After all, it is only in very recent years that the notion of the aggressively sexual, predatory male has come under serious, unsentimentalised scrutiny in any genuinely consequential way. And even in these 'enlightened' times, it is still possible for the prime minister of Great Britain's serial infidelity, not to mention the random fathering of children he then chooses not to acknowledge, to earn him the laurel of 'veteran swordsman' in a major UK newspaper – a title doled out admiringly by the writer and, presumably, with a straight face. While class was obviously a factor in this particular scenario – no cries of 'Deadbeat Dad' for members of the upper echelons of British society – it remains an extraordinary and outrageous indictment of a system of thought and behaviour which considers such men to exist above and beyond the tawdry concepts of honesty, loyalty and responsibility.

It would be disingenuous to express surprise, however, when even the most cursory glance at a reality TV show will usually reveal a whole host of participants striving to emulate the value most strongly associated with the 'alpha male – a willingness to do 'whatever it takes' to come out on top – but also revelling in the possibility of undermining, undercutting and generally devouring the other contestants in one way or another, whenever the opportunity presents itself. This attitude of crass superiority towards others is also one which possesses innumerable reflections. In the rapacious commercial world, it is abundantly clear that a readiness to operate out of this same gross ingestiveness is still regarded as not only a necessary but a laudable, even desirable, quality. Again, there is no point in feigning shock. In our times, as in all times, horror stories of the rich and powerful who have exploited their influence for personal, financial and political gain are legion and equalled only by their, for the most part, infamous ability to avoid significant negative consequences. From the Pharaohs to contemporary financiers, the history of the world has largely been constructed by and around those whose institutionalised, parasitic sense of entitlement and self-regard have permitted them to operate outside the rule of law and beyond ethical and moral considerations. All that is useful and pleasant in the world is their meat and drink, and theirs alone, while what havoc is wreaked in the wake of their avaricious consumption, is invariably left for someone else to clear up. Bernie Madoff may be the notable exception by having ended up behind bars, but the many bankers and hedge funders responsible for the great financial crash of 2008 are still abroad and at their work, even as the political fruits of their greed continue to pervert the course of Western democracy.

At this juncture it may then prove useful to return again to Marina Warner's 'Cannibal Tales', not least because Warner casts a baleful eye across lazy cultural stereotyping and suggests we look beyond the meat we are readily being offered to a more nuanced understanding of the flesh which is frequently hidden behind. Warner's contention is that actual, factual cannibalism, as we have been encouraged to think of it in the West since the beginning of the colonial era – primitive, barbaric, brown people boiling intrepid, well-meaning white missionaries in large pots – never truly existed. In fact, her argument is that colonialist denunciations of native cannibalism served as nothing more than a fig leaf for diverting attention from the colonialists' own acts of barbarity towards those they had colonised. This method of downgrading the humanity, the capacity for emotion – and therefore for suffering – of those they had enslaved and exploited, served the very practical purpose of stanching any inclination towards sympathy or empathy from those back home. Naturally enough, it was particularly important to keep onside all who may have been in a position to agitate against colonial atrocities or for the curtailment of the colonial companies' commercial and political activities. So, rather like the disgust-based campaigns waged against the bodies of women, the colonialists' lurid, and unsubstantiated, tales of vicar soup nurtured the far more productive reaction in their home societies of a deep disgust at the all too evident animality present in these 'cannibal societies'. In turn this led to widespread support for urgently reforming them along 'civilised' and 'Christian' lines. This is Warner's description of why such a seemingly unlikely tactic had the power it did:

Cannibalism helped to justify the presence of the invader, the settler, the trader, bringing civilisation. The centre has to draw outlines to give itself definition. The city has need of the barbarians to know what it is. The self needs the other to establish a sense of integral identity. If my enemies are like me, how can I go on feeling enmity against them?

BECAUSE YOU'RE WORTH IT!

So, while nowadays the tales of 'actual' cannibalism may be viewed with the same degree of suspicion and abhorrence as so many of the 'great deeds' of the empire builders past, its metaphorical usefulness remains potent. In this analogy the 'native' cannibal is now the 'other', is now those who have been set up to fail in order that civilisation can continue to believe in the rightness of its own inhumane progress. The invaders, the settlers and the traders get to both surround the 'native' and define them. Also, because the problem is systemic rather than haphazard, sometimes the 'other' is given a functioning role within the civilising process, serving purposes of which even they may remain unaware.

The 'Keeping Up with the Kardashians' phenomenon might be a case in point. In it, already wealthy, socially advantaged young women seem to advertise the wonders of an unproductive life which celebrates unnecessary weight loss, obsession with perfecting personal appearance and strict adherence to female sexual stereotypes, all reinforcing the notion that these are the only matters that need enter a woman's pretty little head. Of course, the reality behind the 'reality' is the forging of considerable financial empires by each of the Kardashian sisters, but even these dubious ethics are not what the show trades on. Instead women are sold the enviable/unenviable vision of stupidity, vanity and selfishness as an aspirational goal. So, lots of good work put in for the patriarchy there with nary a glimpse of subversion in sight.

Perhaps this attitude too has fed into the hard-selling and overt glamorisation of certain varieties of the alpha male? His enviability – along with the revulsion he has only so very recently started to generate – has been a handy torch to shine in our collective eyes. Because as long as energy and attention are drawn to the glaring examples of so-called 'toxic masculinity' – the presidents and prime ministers, supreme court judges and movie moguls, etc. – the more discreet versions, who are running companies or pulling strings on social media out of the public eye, are freed up to go about the business of exploiting sex-based inequalities for profit, if not completely unhindered certainly with a greater degree of impunity as a result. In pursuit of this, they fill the world with a particular type of noise, which mostly serves either to drown out the sound of opposition or to belittle its concerns. Indeed, one of the great sports of our era has become the drive to popularise and glamorise the meatification of the human body for both entertainment and financial purposes. While it is certainly the case that the range of this activity has now begun to intrude upon the previously sanctified realm of the male body, when it comes to being reduced to the sum of their body parts, women remain the primary target. In their 2008 study 'Women as Sex Objects and Victims in Print Advertisements', the authors, Julie M. Stankiewicz and Francine Rosselli, examined 1,988 advertisements from a mix of fifty-eight popular female- and male-orientated US magazines, including *Elle*, *Vogue*, *Glamour*, *Esquire*, *GQ* and *Men's Health*, and found that 51.8% of advertisements featuring women portrayed them as sex objects, and when looking exclusively at male-orientated magazines this figure rose to 75.98%. From this they drew the implication that:

The fact that it is women who are sexualized in magazines geared toward both men and women indicates that women's bodies are constantly on display to be judged. When women are portrayed as sex objects in two of three images, the message to both men and women is clear: A woman's value lies largely in terms of her appearance and sexuality. In addition, women are things to be looked at, rather than actors with their own sexual desire. Viewing women primarily as objects, useful only for the gratification of men, may in turn make sexual violence against women appear justifiable.

This affects the women working to produce these magazines too, with the Women's Media Centre Speech Project reporting that:

- Close to two-thirds of women journalists report experiencing threats, sexist abuse, intimidation and harassment in the course of doing their work.
- Women journalists also report that more than 25% of the 'verbal, written and/or physical intimidation including

threats to family or friends' they receive happens online.

- 21.1% of surveyed women journalists report experiencing digital/online account surveillance.
- 20.3% of women journalists report email or other digital/online account hacking.

AGEING BEEF: FACTS & FICTION

The sole concession women appear to have been granted, in the face of the seemingly endless barrage of abuse, is the gratuitous displays of ass-covering media savvy which are now served up alongside the jibes and criticisms, as though by the pronouncement of a few magic words that which is being perpetrated against the woman in question will be transformed from a calculated act of dehumanisation into a kindly suggestion or carefully reasoned, and entirely reason-able, moral corrective. Delivered in the risk-averse vocabulary of pop psychology, self-help and so-called 'mindfulness', these duty-bound civilisers profess to be merely interested in 'raising awareness' or stimulating 'debate around the issue'. A recent example is the 2019 column by the former editor of *British Vogue*, Alexandra Shulman, which appeared in the *Daily Mail* under the headline 'I'm sorry Helena Christensen, you ARE too old to wear that'. Accompanied by a photograph of the glamorous-looking supermodel arriving at a party in a black bustier, Shulman opined that, at the age of fifty, Christensen was just 'too old' to be wearing it. Part of Shulman's – apparently completely serious – justification was the line 'When women's bodies no longer serve any child-bearing purpose, we find flaunting them disturbing and slightly tragic. I don't claim that this is fair. But it's true' – the classic 'I didn't say it. I'm just repeating it' defence again. 'As a society,' she went on, 'we are frightened of sexuality that doesn't come accompanied by fertility.' This assertion was carefully caveated with an explanation of how this was, sadly of course, different for 'wrinklies' like the actor Richard Gere and Rolling Stone Ronnie Wood, because despite both having hit their seventh decade, being the parents of small children was proof their fertility was still intact. Content with offering neither argument nor evidence that Helena Christensen's fertility was no longer intact, Shulman also seemed to ignore the question as to whether or not her same logic should be applied to people of any age who may find themselves to be infertile whether through illness or accident? What of those who have made a conscious decision to be sterilised? Presumably, Shulman wouldn't have dreamed of publicly chastising a similarly attired 25-year-old whose chronic endometriosis meant she would probably never bear children of her own. Neither did she bother to address how closely her argument sails to the Catholic Church's taboo on non-procreative sex, which has always played such a significant role in its ongoing campaign against contraception and the protections and freedoms it affords women, and poorer women particularly. Instead she appears to enact a profound innocence about the fact that, by using her very public platform to recycle such achingly clichéd criticisms of middle-aged women, she was party to propagating the problem which she herself claimed to find unfair.

To the slew of complaints which arrived hot on the high heels of the article's publication, along with the numerous declarations of support for Christensen voiced by members of the public and celebrities alike, Shulman offered the, apparently irony-free, defence that she was merely attempting to stir up debate on ageist sexism. To the outside eye, however, it looked rather more like Shulman had unexpectedly found herself caught out in the act of punishing Christensen for refusing to remain within the confines of her socially assigned role – former beauty queen who should now be at home with a rich husband and a squad of children calling herself 'blessed' for domestic bliss having saved her from the horrors of international success, adulation and probably more offers of sex than she could take up in a lifetime.

More specifically, by Christensen publicly daring to venture over to the wrong side of ye olde boundary – through her continued wearing of clothing which might suggest she remains a sexual being/simply put on a top she liked without considering it to be suggestive of anything significant about her at all – it was suddenly permissible for her body to no longer be viewed as the physical manifestation of herself. Instead, she could now be evaluated like a slab of meat which, its quality being found wanting, needed to be returned to the unlovely off-cuts tray.

All of this had to happen, and publicly happen, so that the fixed and familiar order could again regard itself as secure. While some might be inclined to make the argument that public scrutiny of one's body is part and parcel of a model's life, I would direct their attention to the fact that models in the modern era have continuously been used as a stick to beat every other kind of women with. They represent ideals of physical perfection which all other women are measured against and necessarily found to be wanting as a result. Criticism, therefore, of the physical appearance of a model is merely a double serving of the stick for the average woman, with perhaps a taste of schadenfreude thrown in for good measure. It's doubtful any woman reading Shulman's invective imagined it was being aimed at Christensen alone anyway. She seemed to be making it clear to middle-aged women everywhere that exhibiting their peri-menopausal selves in public in anything less than an anti-bingo-wing burka would *not* be without consequence. After all, my God, were women to suddenly reject the idea that middle age, and the body which accompanies it, is synonymous with arriving at an irreversible state of shame, what societal madness might not ensue?

COUNTER-INTELLIGENCE?

History and recent history abound with similar attacks and justifications. In 2008, more than a decade before Shulman's article – and with either the same lack of self-awareness or just an astounding degree of brass-necked cynicism – Julian Linley, the former editor of *Heat* magazine, notorious for its use of invasive paparazzi shots, salacious objectification and targeted mockery of perceived imperfections in the bodies of famous women, offered up the following quote in an interview with the *Guardian* about his time on the magazine: 'Women are objectified constantly in the papers and I think there is something fun and subversive about turning that on its head in a way that isn't trashy.'

How magazine covers bearing the headlines 'Biggest Celebrity Bellies', 'The No Knickers Girls! Who does it – and why?' or 'Stars Fatten Up!' don't count as 'trashy' or somehow manage to act as agents of feminist subversion within the massed ranks of media misogyny, remains unclear because if it doesn't look like subversion and it doesn't quack like subversion ... More to the point, what of the women themselves whose images were splashed so illustratively across the magazine's covers? How much input did they get into how they performed their assigned roles as counter-cultural subversives? The answer remains unknown, unlike the deliberately unflattering photographs of them in various states of undress whose publication, it must be assumed, they were rarely, if ever, given the opportunity to veto.

So, it appears that although paying lip service to the overriding social importance of using women's bodies to score points with – or off – has now become a necessary part of commentators' jobs, the underlying message of Lester Bangs remains firmly in place. All that has changed since his hallowed times then is the speed and reach with which the message can now be spread. The seemingly irresistible impulse to 'meatify' or encourage the idea of the female body as being in some way naturally contaminated – and therefore disgusting – remains the same. It is the impulse behind the unspoken, and yet palpably ubiquitous, decree that young girls be ogled as though they are already young women – the *Sun* and *Sunday Sport*'s countdown to actress Emma Watson and singer Charlotte Church turning sixteen, anyone? That middle-aged women should do all in their power to still appear to be young women – while never fooling themselves or others that they can succeed in being anything other than grotesquely middle-aged. That older women should hide the horrifying impossibility of their ever again being young women in the nearest available operating theatre. And that young women themselves are, in fact, too thin, too fat, too hairy, too stupid, too clever, too ungrateful, too drunk, too uptight, too slutty, too frigid, too fertile, too unconcerned about the length of their reproductive window, too over- and under-educated, too ambitious, too career-minded, too masculine, too androgynous and too feminine for their views about anything – particularly about what it means to be a young woman in such a world – to be taken seriously at all.

Even this degree of engagement only really occurs with young, white, middle-class women. Every other kind of young woman tends to be disappeared into a nebulous conglomeration of clichés about her race and class. However, women of all varieties need only randomly open any magazine, website or social media platform to be speedily apprised of the fact that there is, without question, something very wrong with them and it is expected they will get on to fixing that, immediately. The who and what of their lives, desires and personalities, specifics of their communities and ethnic origins, career status or family situations are not factors which are permitted influence in these judgements. Rather, as will be made just as swiftly clear, the fundamental facts of their lives will not be taken into account at all.

So, it seems that one may only be the right kind of woman or the wrong kind of woman, although the right kind of woman seems to be pretty hard to find. More specifically, this means the meatifiers expect that the meat secretly knows itself for what it is and tacitly agrees to perform all the tasks of meat to the best of its ability. The notion of the female body as meat has been so widely disseminated and comprehensively accepted, over so many generations and across countless eras of social and political upheaval that even now, whenever the meat reveals itself as not only conscious – and conscious of the inequities to which it is being subjected – but also unwilling to accept the grill, it can still cause pandemonium.

The Australian academic and author Jill Conway, writing in her 1970 article 'Stereotypes of Femininity in a theory of Sexual Evolution', commented on the stultification in the Victorian era of any advancement in the intellectual attitude towards women and their perceived roles in society:

> Once environmental factors were removed as major sources of variation, evolutionary theorists were compelled to look for other explanations of the supposed psychic differences between the sexes and other ways to explain the undoubted social fact of the inferiority of women.

And then, as now:

> No matter how the new social science changed its methods, biology remained the determinant of female functions, and sex roles were interpreted according to the accepted values of contemporary social convention.

We cannot think differently about women because women cannot be different to how we think about them, seems to be the depressingly familiar refrain. As the colonialists have taught us, he who creates the most compelling narrative wins and the narrative of those who win becomes not only difficult to dislodge but highly influential to how those lorded over come to view, understand and speak about themselves. If the context through which we experience the world permits only the narrowest possibilities of alternative interpretation, how does this affect not only how we express ourselves but who we eventually become?

BEING SEEN AND HEARD

While a definitive answer to the question of how people become who and what they are may extend slightly beyond my area of expertise, it doesn't seem unreasonable to suggest that the pressure created by the increasingly visual nature of our culture plays some part in it. In his book *Sensual Relations: engaging the senses in culture and social theory*, the anthropologist David Howes writes:

'Sight and hearing were traditionally linked with intellectual activity and civilised behaviour in European culture, while taste, touch and smell were associated with animality.'

Given how male-dominant the civilising roles of publisher, commissioner, curator, programmer of arts institutions and entertainment venues, critic and retailer, etc., have been, it's not surprising that our culture usually bestows greater visibility on male artists, writers and musicians, etc. A depressing recent example being the Abbey Theatre in Dublin – Ireland's national theatre and recipient of half of the entire country's public funding for theatre – and the announcement of their 'Waking the Nation' season to commemorate the centenary of Ireland's landmark 1916 Uprising. Of the ten plays announced, nine were written by men, and of the ten directors announced, only three were women. Outrage at this wilful exclusion of women, by a prominent national institution from an important national conversation, provoked the launch of the 'Waking the Feminists' campaign which challenged this gross misuse of public subsidy. Of course, the Abbey Theatre was only the latest in a long line of institutions to unquestioningly indulge its androcentrism. The supposed taste for male leads, and male-centred narratives, which are habitually deemed to be more in tune with the interests of male audiences – who, apparently, have as little curiosity in films and plays about, and by, women as they have in reading their books – means the commissioners for these types of platforms regularly consign female characters and storylines to secondary, supporting status.

Similarly, sportswomen and female sporting associations still struggle to gain anything like recognition for their achievements, parity of marketing spend and salary equality with their male counterparts, from broadcasters and sporting organisations alike – particularly in the traditionally male team sports. For instance, in 2015 the US women's soccer team won the World Cup and, as a result, generated $20 million more in revenue than their male counterparts. However, they received the equivalent of only a quarter of the male players' salaries, a disparity so galling it obliged the team to launch a gender discrimination lawsuit against US Soccer. But even the flagrant discrimination of long-established cultural and sporting institutions are far outweighed by those perpetrated by the giant media and tech moguls who nowadays control our culture's public face and have nurtured its growth in their image with, until very recently, a free hand. Rupert Murdoch's apparent resentment at having to remove Roger Ailes from his post as CEO of Fox News, after allegations of his long history of sexual abuse and harassment of female staff grew too clamorous to be ignored, seems all too evident in the $45 million payout with which he put Ailes out to pasture in 2016. And in 2020 an open letter was sent to Mark Zuckerberg, accusing him of allowing Facebook to destroy the reputations of female politicians, with one of its signatories, film-maker Baroness Beeban Kidron, stating, 'Women fought for generations to hold public office – Facebook is enabling those who would push us backwards.'

The evolution of media and technology from print to the predominantly visual/image-based format is a significant change in a society where, traditionally, not only children but women were already best seen and not heard. Because, where print requires at least a basic level of active engagement from the reader, and subsequent exercise of critical function no matter how paltry, the response to imagery is instantaneous and therefore more likely to be emotion- or 'instinct'-based. For purveyors of the disgust myth, the invention of the inter-net as a platform for the rapid, widespread dissemination of images which can never truly be recalled, and which offer interpre-tations that can never be properly refuted, was a game-changer. This remains the case despite the fact we, their avid consumers, are no longer naive enough to believe that the information they pass on to us arrives bias-free. We know that everything we see has already been filtered through whichever agenda our chosen outlet has thrown their lot in with. We also know plenty about the media's targeted use of imagery to manipulate emotion in order to make viewers more susceptible to particular narratives, which debunks any argument that this is an unfortunate, inadvertent, side effect of the medium rather than active and targeted political choice.

At its inception, social media seemed to be a noble experiment in finding more unmediated ways for people to represent themselves and to communicate with others. By circumventing the old official channels, it could return the power of what is seen and heard of ourselves to ourselves, allowing the unrefined truth to out. In reality, it has only served to hasten the drip down of misinformation and misrepresentation into everyday life. But perhaps social media's failure to foster more meaningful human interactions lies not in the nature of the technologies themselves – although the revelation of their unauthorised use in detaching us from our personal information for commercial and political exploitation has proved yet another catastrophic disappointment of their potential. Perhaps instead it lies in our deeply ingrained cultural conditioning which continues to operate through them, subverting the better intentioned efforts to connect us with each other in deeper or less moderated ways. Unhappily, the specifically visual platform, Instagram, has turned out to be little more than a measure of the effort we are willing to exert in order to avoid our lives eliciting the dread disgust. Here we demonstrate how well we can coordinate our breakfasts with our moods, stage-manage 'treasured' moments of intimacy and curate embarrassing gaffes into hilarious mishaps, while image filters busily relieve us of physical imperfections or even physical reality, and all, presumably, to keep the ever-present risk of meatification at bay. This seems to entail expending an unwarranted amount of anxiety and energy on a platform which, at its outset, was just supposed to be fun. But, of course, no one can delude themselves any more about the huge influence images now carry with them and the danger attached to their distribution, depending on who gets to wield that power. This is rarely more disturbingly evident than in cases of so-called 'revenge porn'.

STOP HITTING YOURSELF!

When this particular abuse is perpetrated, not only does the woman in question have to bear the humiliation of the sexual act which she – in the best-case scenario – has consented to the recording of on the understanding it is to be used for private purposes alone being made public for malicious ones, she is also forced to experience her own body's public pornification and meatification. Her right to moderate access to images of her body has been deliberately removed from her domain for the gratification, entertainment, mockery and vilification of those for whom such images were never intended. The further bitter irony, of course, is that the victim is usually held responsible for the situation occurring in the first place. The choruses of 'Well, what did you expect?' and 'It's your own fault for allowing yourself to be photographed/filmed in a compromising position', which are the more voluble accompaniment to these occurrences than expressions of sympathy or outrage at the behaviour of the perpetrator, only make the defilement harder to bear. It is, after all, the intent of such responses to show that by failing to retain control of how she is seen, the woman in question has in some way incited this assault and should, rightly, be shamed for it. Also dispiriting is how often these responses come from other women.

While this might appear somewhat irrational, the patriarchy has always had its useful fools; those willing to race out and ensure they are seen to be its creature and do its bidding. And those useful fools have always come from both camps. What willing men gain from their alignment is self-evident; why women so frequently climb on the bandwagon has always been a little more bewildering and a lot more depressing. Perhaps it's a calculated attempt to align with power in order to be afforded its protections? If so, then it's a childish act of self-deception for, whatever one does or whoever one sides with, the stain of being a woman is indelible and the dangers accruing from that point on can't be outrun. The 'Well, wear trousers then' attitude slung at the campaigner Gina Martin in her efforts to have a law making illegal the noxious practice of upskirting – the illicit taking of photographs of the underwear or genitalia of skirt wearers – is another example of the ways in which women are habitually regarded to be the architects of their own meatification.

Martin's campaign was set in train when,

while standing in a crowded public park at a music festival, she noticed a man in front of her looking at upskirt shots on his phone. On closer inspection she realised that the shots were, in fact, of herself. On bringing the matter to the attention of the police, she was informed that, as she was in a public place at the time and upskirting was not a specific offence, beyond requesting that the man himself delete the pictures, there could be no further action taken. By this somewhat tortured logic then, women in public places have no right or reason to expect their bodily integrity and privacy to be respected even while on the inside of their own clothes. Not only is this both enraging and alarming, it is also indicative of the state of personal purdah to which women in all societies are expected to willingly submit themselves. Fortunately, the lack of existing recourse to legal redress spurred Martin on to mount her, ultimately successful, campaign.

However, its precedent was another powerful example of how baseline societal expectation remains that not only must women constantly police how their bodies look, what their bodies do, images of their bodies and the whereabouts of those images of their bodies, they must also police their magical gift for inciting men into inappropriate, illegal or violatory attempts to remove images of those bodies from their purview. In other words, it's a woman's job to ensure men don't behave like scumbags or get publicly called to account for behaving like scumbags. As long as this wilful misdirection of responsibility soldiers on, women will continue to be held accountable for their exploitation and victimisation, and should they claim otherwise, there will be unpleasant consequences. Again, the daily rape and murder threats openly levelled at women on Twitter are ample evidence of this inglorious truth.

Of course, examples of victims of sexual assault being blamed for the crimes perpetrated against them date all the way back through history to classical antiquity. The rape of Lucretia by Sextus Tarquinus in 510 BC, followed by her suicide which, according to the Roman historian Livy, resulted from her fear of being accused of complicity in the crime, set something of a standard. Sadly, it's hard to imagine outrage at a royal rapist leading to the overthrow of a monarchy today – although the allegations of having sex with a trafficked minor (surely, statutory rape at the very least?) being levelled against Prince Andrew at the time of writing, as well as his dismissal from public life as a direct result, make for interesting viewing ...

Another example is the now notorious remark made by a Toronto police constable, Michael Sanguinetti, which led to the creation of the SlutWalk movement in 2011. While addressing a safety forum about rape prevention on campus, Sanguinetti said, 'I've been told I'm not supposed to say this...' before continuing, 'however, women should avoid dressing like sluts in order not to be victimized.' Closer to home, in 2019, the Welsh

Secretary, Alun Cairns, was forced to resign for feigning ignorance about the Conservative Party employee and Welsh Assembly candidate Ross England who deliberately sabotaged a rape trial by making false claims about the victim's sexual history. Amazingly, the Cabinet Office inquiry found that Cairns had not breached the ministerial code, leading the woman in question to describe the inquiry as 'a sham'. Around the same time, over in Norfolk, the Conservative Party had just selected Nick Conrad as their candidate for the Broadland constituency despite his lengthy explanation on Radio Norfolk in 2014 as to why women are 'partially responsible' for rape and advising that any woman not wanting to be raped had 'best probably keep your knickers on'. In this instance, at least, the ensuing outcry meant Conrad had to step down, although not before the prime minister, Boris Johnson, had made a point of publicly noting that Conrad had apologised for the comments 'long ago'.

BUT HE HAS A VERY,
VERY GOOD JOB...

How victim-blaming scenarios play out in court, and in the media, is all too wearyingly familiar.

However, the specific taboo on women failing to control imagery of themselves is a very recent, significant pushing back of the border between meat and flesh. After all, where once Samuel Pepys could only have dreamed of being one of the lucky few invited to view Peter Lely's semi-nude portrait of Barbara Villiers – or Nell Gwyn, depending on who you believe – that Charles II kept hidden behind a secret panel in his bed chamber, nowadays a few quick clicks are all that's required to turn a private body into an object of public display which then remains available to view anywhere, at any time and by anyone, permanently.

So, although the roots of this attitude may be ancient, we know we are witnessing the inception of a new taboo in response to a new technology, and legislation has yet to catch up.

Even when legislation does catch up, as in the case of the eventual passing of the upskirting law, the culture of disregarding or diminishing the seriousness of the crime persists. For example, in the summer of 2019, a 24-year-old man, Michael Chan, was stopped by a security guard in Topshop on Oxford Street, for hanging around and behaving suspiciously with a phone towards a woman shopping. When it was discovered that the phone held more than 1,700 upskirting images, Chan was charged with outraging public decency. Defending him, Michael Magarian QC first sought to mitigate the sentence by informing the magistrate that, as an accountant at Price-waterhouseCoopers, his client has 'a very, very good job'. He followed this up by suggesting that the offence itself wasn't really that serious because the women photographed had remained unaware of Chan's activities. However, the prosecutor Malachy

Pakenham argued: 'To say there is no harm I disagree with. If women wearing skirts have a fear or trepidation that men near them may use devices to record them then that will have an impact on society. Courts when they sentence reflect the errors of society and the fact these women did not know what he was doing does not go in his favour at all. If the harm was non-existent it wouldn't be a criminal offence, would it?'

Happily, in this case, the magistrate, Victoria Readman, not only concurred but forwarded Chan's case to Southwark Crown Court where, she believed, he would receive a harsher sentence than she was legally allowed to mete out. Ultimately this proved to be so, and in November 2019, Chan was sentenced to an eight-month suspended prison sentence, a five-year Sexual Harm Prevention order and ordered to attend a hundred days of a programme for male sex offenders. While this outcome was certainly a welcome result for women, the use of the upskirter's implied high social status – via his 'very,

very good job' – followed by the suggestion that upskirting is, essentially, a victimless crime, is demoralising. It's impossible to imagine anyone arguing the harmlessness of similarly, intimately intrusive surveillance of non-consenting individuals when it was perpetrated by organisations like the Stasi or the CIA or even, today, by members of the paparazzi. But apparently, it's still worth arguing the toss when such activities have been embarked upon by men who have a 'very, very good job'.

HARLOTS: THE REBOOT

Women, then, who possess no such natural immunity to consequences, occupy a very different position in society and are subject to an alternative set of taboos that have been instituted by – to quote Mary Douglas – 'leading members of the society' and 'controllers of opinion'. In this instance, the taboo seems to have been laid across the back of any woman who can be seen with the naked eye. By dint of this basic visibility, she is automatically existing in a place larger than the boundaries of her own physical space. She has become the dreaded 'matter out of place' and is, therefore, guilty of taking up valuable public room which would otherwise be reserved for attention to men and male concerns. Again, one need only glance at the Twitter feeds of any prominent woman, or indeed any woman expressing an opinion about anything at all, to see the vehement, violent and often totally illogical reactions she elicits from the online trolls. These would-be 'controllers of opinion' are readily identifiable by their seething, infantile rages, rape and murder threats over even minor matters of disagreement, and inappropriately emotional/ intellectually nonsensical contentions – in recent years this has expanded to include a profound sense of their own victimisation, even when in the midst of trying to publicly destroy the woman in question's career or reputation. For example, anyone with even a passing interest in such things knew that upon the announcement of the actress Brie Larson in the lead role of the new 'Captain Marvel' film, she and the whole enterprise were about to be fallen upon by hordes of whining incels. And, sure as night follows day, the influential review aggregator Rotten Tomatoes had to make major alterations to its rules to counteract the site's bombardment by misogynist trolls, attempting – unsuccessfully – to adversely affect the film's box office returns.

But how can this taboo, of allowing oneself to be seen, extend to women who are victims of revenge porn or upskirting, both activities which absolutely depend upon the women involved neither actively participating nor consenting? Perhaps the aggression and lack of sympathy shown to victims of these crimes illustrates where the new taboos interlink with the old, the notion of the 'respectable woman' versus the 'harlot'. The 'respectable woman' of the Victorian tradition would not dream of allowing herself to be 'seen' and indeed, supposedly, took every possible action to avoid drawing public attention to herself, while the 'harlot' made her living by her very visibility – the term 'harlot' of course extending, in the popular imagination, far beyond women who were literally working in prostitution, to include those engaged in any manner of public-facing, non-professional employment and applied particularly to performers involved in any but the most exalted kind of artistic endeavour. In the UK today, where women may not only legally stand in any public park of their choosing unaccompanied by chaperons and therefore without 'cover', they are also, and legally, the sole monitors of what they wear, how they conduct themselves and what company they keep while doing so. This appears to have been interpreted, by some 'controllers of opinion', as women electing to make 'matter out of place' of themselves.

In choosing to become the new 'harlots', the deciders of their own fate – also recognisable by their tendency to publicly revel in, and reclaim, their denunciation as 'nasty' persisting dissenters – women make themselves fair game for the rejected boyfriend, the revenge pornographer and the avid upskirter, as well as, in many cases, the law itself which has been put in place by primarily male lawmakers to guard against the deleterious effects of female insubordination. So, like the poor and taxes, it appears the Victorians are always with us.

The double bind, in which contemporary women's very independence serves as a trigger for new technology to be put to old use – and thereby giving birth to a brand-new taboo – is neatly summed up by the French philosopher and social theorist Michel Foucault, in 'The cycle of prohibition' section of his 1976 work *The History of Sexuality, 1: The Will to Knowledge*:

thou shalt not go near, thou shalt not touch, thou shalt not consume, thou shalt not experience pleasure, thou shalt not speak, thou shalt not show thyself; ultimately thou shalt not exist, except in darkness and secrecy. To deal with sex, power employs nothing more than a law of prohibition. Its objective: that sex renounce itself. Its instrument: the threat of punishment that is nothing other than the suppression of sex. Renounce yourself or suffer the penalty of being suppressed; do not appear if you do not want to disappear. Your existence will be maintained only at the cost of your nullification. Power constrains sex through a taboo that plays on the alternative between two nonexistences.

And so, women's unwillingness to cooperate with the old taboos, which equate 'being seen' with a lack of 'respectability', can be interpreted as the wilful putting of themselves in a position where the self-appointed border guards of the patriarchy may 'legitimately' be moved to correct their erroneous assumption of possessing a right to control the production and dispersal of images of their own bodies. The development of this new standard seems to have conveniently coincided with the arrival of digital photography, only made worse by the advent of the camera-phone which permitted the creation, storing and sharing of photographic images with unprecedented freedom and economy. Once the new taboo became firmly embedded in the culture, however, women who transgressed it (i.e. most women) – through acting on their clearly unaffirmed belief that the business of their bodies was their own – were automatically deemed to be merely exposing the truth of what has always been suspected of them: that women possess an essential streak of animality which makes them unfit for the decent 'respectable' treatment their male peers can take as a given. This being the case then, women putting themselves in positions where, even unauthorised, transfers of control of these 'higher sense' aspects of their lives occur, choose to dwell beyond the bounds of sympathy or right of redress. In the best-case scenario, they are viewed as stooges, duped into colluding in their own exploitation at the hands of those advanced beings clever enough to have seen both gratification and currency where women themselves, apparently, saw only self.

The chilling, practical, day-to-day implementation of this means that all women live under the active threat of being stripped of their personal autonomy and dignity in any place and at any time. The truth of this was much in evidence in August 2019 when widespread protests erupted in Seoul against the tide of 'molka' films – covert filming of women with the footage subsequently uploaded to subscription websites – flooding the internet. The protesters' banners read 'My Life is not your Porn'. Two months later a young Korean woman, unable to recover from the humiliation of discovering that a man had preyed upon her in this manner while she was in a hospital changing room, took her own life. So the fear of this does not arise from an idle or imagined potential threat but an actual, active one which can and does have real and lasting consequences for its victims.

PHOTOGRAPHING THE THING

'To photograph is to appropriate the thing photographed. It means putting oneself into a certain relation to the world that feels like knowledge – and, therefore, like power,' wrote Susan Sontag in her 1977 essay *On Photography.* An obvious inversion of her argument, then, is that to be the thing photographed is also to be put into a certain – if somewhat different – relation to the world, one that feels like ignorance and, therefore, like weakness. A camera is a predatory weapon, she contends, in much the same way a car is, and while no one has ever been literally photographed to death, it certainly raises the spectre of the paparazzi hounding Diana, Princess of Wales.

'Still, there is something predatory in the

act of taking a picture,' Sontag continues. 'To photograph people is to violate them, by seeing them as they can never see themselves, by having knowledge of them they can never have; it turns people into objects that can be symbolically possessed.'

Although these lines were written before the vast technological changes which less than twenty years later would again alter ideas about the ownership, meaning and control of imagery, Sontag's theory still fits. Indeed, the manner in which graphically explicit hardcore pornography would flood through the world's computers into every connected home, serves only to compound her point.

LUCKY, LUCKY LIBERTINES

Of course, in whichever ways the manner and means of distribution have been revolutionised in recent years, pornography itself in one form or another is nothing new. The roots of what we are able to recognise as 'modern' pornography are thought to lie in the 'libertine' literature of the seventeen century. Written by men, for men, its creators often adopted a female narrative perspective in order to make whatever was about to befall the female bodies in question more acceptable – see also: 'She wanted it', 'She secretly wanted it', 'She loved it', 'She secretly loved it', etc. and ad nauseam. Much of this literature then, like the libertines who wrote and used it, was unambiguously misogynistic, with women reduced to receptacles whose sole purpose was the provision of male sexual satisfaction – a tradition which continues on in the majority of pornography to this day. It's probably worth noting that this was also the period in which a defined separation of sex from procreation began to establish itself in the popular male imagination. Once it became accepted that sex could, and should, be an activity for men to enjoy as a consequence-free end in itself, all that remained was for the women, who inescapably bore all repercussions – the unwanted pregnancies, single parenthood and the damaging loss of reputation – to be relegated to so lowly a status as to make it permissible to dismiss them from the mind as easily as from the bed.

In life, as in literature, the identifiably sexual woman became an object of disgust – a thing out of place. As the urban, capitalist, industrial and middle-class world came into being over the nineteenth century, sexuality became increasingly hived off from the rest of life. So too did the now medical obsession with curtailing masturbation in children, and the social measures used to enforce the frigidification of the 'respectable' woman. All the while, for nineteenth-century men sexual licence abounded – albeit covertly pursued – and the thriving trade in pornography offered up an intriguingly reversed image of all that Victorian mores were supposed to represent. It seems that as long as the sexual life was structured around heterosexual male pleasure – masturbatory or otherwise – anything went.

Nearly two hundred years later, this attitude remains in the compulsively unrealistic portrayal of female sexual desire apparent in so much contemporary, heterosexually-orientated porn.

'AVIN' A LARF

A great deal has been written about the bitter divide between the 'anti-porn' and 'sex-positive' feminists, but while women may agree or disagree with Robin Morgan's iconoclastic statement that 'Pornography is the theory, and rape is the practice', few would deny that today's multimillion-pound porn industry has built its cathedrals on the bodies of exploited, maltreated and dehumanised people, the overwhelming majority of whom are women. Rather like recognising the folly of blaming technology for the uses to which it has been put, it is tempting to ask if pornography and misogyny are completely inextricable or if porn could be created in a way which would be safe and equitable for its performers and therefore a simpler, guilt-free experience for its consumers? It is, after all, only people engaging in sexual activity for the sexual satisfaction of others. As matters stand, however, the nature of much pornographic content, the conditions under which it is produced, the aggressive, scattergun manner of its distribution and questions about who has access to the resulting material, are all too pressing to set aside for such contemplations. So, while the arguments rattle back and forth about supporting individual freedoms and the importance of not criticising sexual tastes – conveniently creating more heat about the right to persist with consuming exploitative, or abusive, material than light about the potential personal and societal fallout of leaving such matters unchallenged – I cannot help noticing the obstacles over which women are expected to clamber, in order to even ask these questions, have multiplied and proliferated, almost in tandem with the growth of internet porn itself.

Perhaps this is to be expected. It is, after all, only a continuation of the long tradition of regarding women's bodies as possessing an inherently lower status in matters sexual, so why should their opinions on the subject be treated any differently? Again, the difficulty of redressing this imbalance has always been compounded by women traditionally being held in check by disgust's great ally, the morality of shame, while men are more usually held to the, far less personally onerous, morality of guilt.

'Shame morality,' William Ian Miller states in his *Anatomy of Disgust*, 'is more expansive than guilt morality; it cares about what you are as well as what you do; it cares about what you don't do and what you can't do. More becomes blameable. And because more becomes blameable, correlatively more becomes a matter of honor and pride.' This exercise of shame over women has proved as useful in the popularising of passive, lenient attitudes towards internet porn as it has everywhere else in our lives.

Being old enough to remember the before and after of the arrival of internet porn, I recall how rapidly the narrative around its emergence evolved. I remember there being an initial brief period when it suddenly became a frequent topic of conversation among friends, almost a currency by which men could admit to or speak with reasonable openness about their personal use of pornography and their sometimes complicated relationship with it. But hot on its heels an explicitly – and dispiriting – antifeminist narrative began to develop in the lads' mags and tabloid media, as though the previous conversation had really only been about creating a sense of complicity among men, a sort of 'we're all in it together, aren't we?' attitude, whether they actually wanted to be complicit or not. This narrative rapidly gained traction, silenced voices of dissent and created an atmosphere in which women found it impossible to talk about pornography, or the methods of its production, without facing a barrage of jocularly delivered, but deadly serious, accusations of being shrill, humourless spoilsports. And, conveniently, it stuck.

'The pious and pompous preach the perils of porn from the pulpit,' thunders David Ludden, PhD, in a 2018 article in *Psychology Today*, which supposedly examines whether or not porn is harmful to *men*. Imagine my surprise when the article ends with the line: 'I imagine that, in another generation or two, people will wonder what all the fuss was about back in the dark ages of the early 21st century.' Several years after leaving his job as editor of *Loaded* magazine – one of the most successful lads' mags of the nineties – Martin Daubney penned a mea culpa in the *Daily Mail* about his part in assimilating porn into the mainstream. 'We were normalising soft porn, and in so doing we must have made it more acceptable for young men to dive into the murky waters of harder stuff on the internet. And, for that, I have a haunting sense of regret.' In the midst of his chest beating, however, he still managed to include the line: 'There wasn't a month went by when a minor Lib Dem MP or feminist lobby group didn't try to make a name for themselves by demanding we were placed on the top shelf, or banned.' So, while his regret was real, their concern was only a matter of self-promotion ... of course ... But before he arrived at his contrition, my generation of young women were required to think fast and do a lot of catching up in order to get to grips with the wholly new pornographic and highly sexualised landscape we were suddenly presented with.

Placed in an impossible position where we alone were supposed to navigate the choppy waters between freedom of expression and protesting the objectification of women, we found ourselves under tremendous social pressure to ignore, or trivialise, feminist concerns. The lairy 'ladette' culture of the early and mid-1990s was in the process of being shamed into an acceptable lads' mag version in which the gorgeous girls, siding with their fit blokes against the foul

feminists, laughed along at their own meatification for the edification of all. Over time,
the lads' mag girls were dispatched too, to
make way for the 're-girlification' of women.
Ads squealed 'Here come the girls' as hordes
of hysterical women rushed for the make-up
counter, while the 'using hookers is harmless' humour of *Friends* was replaced by
big skirts and always-hot-to-trot-for-sex
'girls' of *Sex and the City*. And, really, when
you thought about it, was there anything
as ugly, obnoxious and unfeminine as all
those women in their power suits back in
the 1980s?

This was where internet porn arrived to
play and 'modern' women were expected to
be savvy enough, and post-feminist enough,
to know that even though it didn't look very
ironic, porn was in on the joke. Unsurpris-
ingly then, finding themselves flanked on
every side by this new 'fun', 'sophisticated'
and above all 'knowing' image of what a
woman should be, actual women found
themselves in a trapped place. In order to

assert their value here as 'real' or 'proper' women – as opposed to 'feminist' women – they were compelled to reject any shared identification with the concerns of feminism or of a female liberation which might threaten these new, and oh-so-speedily standardised, notions of behaviour.

'AND SUCH SMALL PORTIONS'

At the risk of complicating matters, I can't resist pointing out that an additional source of irritation in the midst of all this liberated sexual 'fun' was the total lopsidedness of porn's output from the consumer's point of view. In this regard I can't help thinking of the old, pre-cancellation, joke from Woody Allen's *Annie Hall*: 'Two elderly women are at a Catskill restaurant. One of them says, "Boy, the food at this place is just terrible." The other says, "Yeah I know. And such small portions."' After all, in this great democratisation of sexual pleasure, the sexual pleasure available for women through the use of pornography 1) remained largely un-catered for, and 2) remained an utterly taboo topic of conversation. So, 'Don't be sexual in a way which is not available for men to partake of' became the silent message which ran underneath 'Don't be so uptight' and 'Don't object'. The utterly byzantine nature of all this is typified by the way in which completely hetero-fied versions of lesbian sex have always proved so popular with male users and, for very different reasons, female users as well – presumably because the female body is getting some sort of a look-in when it comes to sexual pleasure. In 2015, Pornhub published a survey in which it announced that the 21–24% of their customers who identified themselves as women, overwhelmingly searched for lesbian and gay sex as a first and second preference. What this suggests about women's views on the quality of porn depicting heterosexual sex requires little unpacking; I'd say a rejection of the 'woman-as-depot' narrative about covers it.

While, more recently, inroads have been

made by female pornographers in creating female-friendly porn, the market for this material remains minuscule and is regarded as far more niche than the porn staples of BDSM, double penetration or 'bukkake'. And over time, the sheen of unrestricted access to porn has become tarnished for men too, and in worse ways than just a resurgence of the old image of porn's habitual users as lonely dirty-mac wearers. There are and have been continued difficulties with stamping out child pornography, as well as catching and penalising those involved in creating and dispersing violent, coercive and revenge pornography. There has been a huge rise in trafficked women being forced into porn, as well as in reports of the personal chaos caused by those trapped in internet porn addictions, and questions about the effect of exposure to pornographic material on the emotional, social and sexual develop-ment of children and adolescents, continue to preoccupy psychologists, sociologists and academics alike. Feminism's age-old anxiety about pornography's role in triggering sexual violence towards women out in the real world as well as promoting and reinforcing destructive gender stereotypes remains.

LADY LOOKS LIKE A LADY

Such stereotypes form the foundation of our culture of female sexual objectification which, far from being on the wane, gives every impression of positively flourishing.

Sexual objectification is no modern invention, of course. In the late eighteenth century, while advocating monogamous marriage as the only true means of circumventing it, the German philosopher Immanuel Kant wrote in his *Lectures on Ethics*:

> sexual love makes of the loved person an Object of appetite; as soon as that appetite has been stilled, the person is cast aside as one casts away a lemon which has been sucked dry ... Taken by itself it

is a degradation of human nature; for as soon as a person becomes an Object of appetite for another, all motives of moral relationship cease to function, because as an Object of appetite for another a person becomes a thing and can be treated and used as such by every one ... The desire which a man has for a woman is not directed towards her because she is a human being, but because she is a woman; that she is a human being is of no concern to the man; only her sex is the object of his desires. Human nature is thus subordinated.

As far as the dictionary definition of objectification goes, its two main meanings are:

1. the action of degrading someone to the status of a mere object.
2. the expression of something abstract in a concrete form.

The meaning of the former seems straight-forward enough. Everyone is familiar with the fetishisation of the female body which, in turn, dissociates it from its accompany-ing humanity. The latter definition is less tangible. I wonder, however, if it also creates a little more space for understanding the complexity of the problem of objectifica-tion. After all, a great deal of power resides in the hands of whoever gets to decide what is abstract in the first place, as well as who then has the majority say over whichever form the abstraction ought to be obliged to take when becoming concrete. 'The body is part of the self,' says Kant, 'in its together-ness with the self it constitutes the person.' The simplicity of this proposition seems self-evident but while a recognised self, which is indivisible from the body it inhabits, has been the basic understanding traditionally accorded to men – white 'alpha males' most particularly – without serious objection ever being raised, this remains a luxury rarely, if ever, afforded to women. Lacan's infamous declaration that 'woman does not exist', which suggested the nature of woman to be fundamentally amorphous, compared to the fixed north of the nature of man – making it, therefore, open to reinterpretation by whosoever wishes to take a stab at it, presumably? – certainly hasn't helped matters. His 'Woman is a symptom of man' is equally problematic, suggesting that women only gain materiality when viewed in relation to men. While I am perhaps playing devil's advocate with these interpretations – Lacan has feminist advocates as well as detractors – it is hard not to read into them a rejection of woman having an existence separate to men's perceptions of them as fantasy objects, motivators of desire, although perhaps also as mothers and caretakers. If this is so, then women's only option is to found all sense of self on their body's capacity to either sexually arouse men or tend to their other needs. This is achieved by dutifully inhabiting, accepting and performing their assigned, stereotypical gender roles, in a manner precisely opposite to male understanding of what selfhood constitutes. Therefore, when women demonstrate an unwillingness to perform, or conform to, these stereotypes, they are transgressing and making of themselves something out of place. While recognising that this imposed gender performance has deep roots in our history, it is alarming that even the increased biological and medical information amassed about the female body in recent years has failed to dislodge it – although it should be added that this information seems to have been mostly gathered in spite of the medical profession's seeming embrace of Lacan's idea that, as men are the baseline of humanity, women's anomalous bodies require no separate research for potentially lifesaving variations in treatment ...

MIRROR, MIRROR

Women's historical struggle against appropriation and objectification looks set to continue then. Adding fuel to this fire is the increasing pressure – from ever earlier ages – on women to engage in self-objectification or, perhaps, subjectification. This enterprise has been jolted into hyperdrive in recent decades by the rise of celebrity culture, reality TV and the cult followings which spring up around the 'famous for being famous'. These in turn have popularised a mode of behaviour fuelled by a longing to emulate the notoriety, financial success and, apparently, glamorous lifestyles of these 'personality and/or outrage' celebrities, who have largely attained this status themselves through a willingness to engage in the ruthless self-commodification and 'personal branding'. From feuds between YouTubers and the cynical financial deals struck with 'Influencers' to the sense of being constantly, and critically, surveilled – an anxiety frequently reported particularly by the generations who have grown up as digital natives and who cannot imagine how it is to live without the continuous, intimate scrutiny of their peers and complete strangers alike – it is now dispiritingly common to hear teenagers and young people enthuse about 'their brand'. Or talk about the effort required to protect and promote these narrow, idealised versions of themselves as though it was a cause for celebration rather than a prison of their own making.

But even this contemporary 'branding' issue is surely just a repackaging of older forms of control. For countless generations, women have been walled up inside 'their brand' and warned to remain there under threat of violence, abuse and social ostracisation.

As human beings are a complex synthesis of biology, environment, belief and capacity for reason, the wider re-designation of what is specific to the bodies of women – female sexual organs, reproductive systems and their ensuing natural functions – from simply being an important component of what it is to be a female human being, into the definitive totality of all a woman is ever permitted to be, was a radical move and a catastrophic event. As the poet, and professor of classics, Anne Carson writes in her investigation of the erotic in Greek literature, 'Putting her in her Place: Woman, Dirt and Desire': 'Since woman does not bound herself, she must be bounded. This is achieved by organization of her space, prescription of her gestures, ordering of her rituals, imposition of headgear, attendants and other trappings.'

Carson's point retains every bit of its pungency when translated to the modern era and taboos imposed by the 'controllers of opinion': if women refuse to be what has been decided for them, they will be forced to comply. Therefore, they must stay within their prescribed roles, remain in their designated places and be obliged to behave in the ways deemed appropriate to them. The correct framework will be provided for their interactions with the male world, they will be compelled to wear what has been approved, socialise in a manner considered fitting to them and generally pass through life without causing ructions to the status quo. The imposed boundary which resulted from this type of thinking brought with it a vastly truncated version of what womanhood could be, or even be perceived to be. So successful was this boundary's establishment it ensured that the intellectual, social and economic components of women's lives – i.e. pretty much every significant aspect of women's lives – would become at best stunted and at worst obliterated, for countless generations to come. And what remained acceptably within a woman's domain – personal appearance, physical experience, the care of children and domestic duties – were also all whittled down to a sharpened point with which to torment her should she dare to make choices, or express preferences, which were not in line with the good upkeep of said boundary. Whichever way you jump, we've got you, was the message and, back in reality, this has indeed proved to be the case.

So, it would seem that, right at the beginning of literature, the mythification of Helen of Troy set the blueprint which simultaneously instigated the adulation of the perfect female face and the abjuration of everything that went on in the brain sitting in the skull behind it.

DOWN THE MARKET

Unhappily for women, the patriarchy has been unflinching and imaginative in reinforcing this myth. Maybe this is why opponents of women's right to assert a full and final say over what happens to their bodies are rarely able to set out their arguments in a reasoned and logical manner? Instead we must all endure the old tropes about God and 'nature' and the 'natural order of things', which permit and encourage deep-rooted, conveniently misogynist traditions to do most of the heavy lifting while physical violence, threats, insults, sexual slurs and wearying, disgust-laden clichés about women and their bodies take care of the rest. Presumably for those who prefer 'their' women barefoot, pregnant, dependent or at the very least silent, this is not a civilised subject, it is a fight to the death – a cultural rather than physical death, probably, but then ... who knows? What we do know is that they suspect, should they happen to lose the argument, the potential for radical change to their everyday lives, and to the society that has always cradled and protected their interests, is so great that the Queensberry Rules no longer hold sway.

Strategically, then, the effort to derail women's struggle against the impositions of their 'brand' has focused on blurring their ability to recognise the difference between what they know themselves to be and how the lenses of objectification oblige them to experience the world. In this context, viewing and treating themselves as meat, rather than flesh, is not only reasonable and rational but precisely the goal they should be striving to attain. It is a method of control notable for its ability to sell women the notion that they are engaging in empowered acts of physical expression while at the same time pressuring them to conform to ever narrowing ideals of what an acceptable female body looks like and how it should express itself.

Sue Tilley, the plus-size life model for the Lucian Freud painting *Benefits Supervisor Sleeping* – in which she is depicted naked, asleep on a couch – once recounted her experience of going to the Whitechapel Gallery to see the painting *in situ* and overhearing a man decrying how fat, revolting and disgusting she was. 'I know I'm not the "ideal woman", I know I'm not,' she said. 'But who is? And he never made the skinny ones look any better.' Be that as it may, it's hard to imagine Kate Moss ever overhearing comparable comments about her Freud portrait.

The fashion, beauty and cosmetic surgery industries have been dedicated to these double standards from the outset, and the film industry has never been far behind, creating hugely influential physical and sexual stereotypes almost from the moment of cinema's inception. The fitness industry has plenty of blood on its hands in this regard too, with its endless workout videos hosted by skinny, scantily clad celebrities.

Notable also is that even when the sportswear giant Nike attempted some redress by, as it did in 2019, displaying its wares on a 'plus-size' mannequin in its flagship London shop, it immediately became the target of a scathing article in the *Telegraph* by journalist Tanya Gold. While questioning the purity of Nike's motives, as is entirely proper whenever big business and women's bodies intersect, the article also featured some odd, unnecessary jibes about the mannequin's size and shape – and, by implication, the women whose size and shape it represented. It was, apparently, 'immense, vast, gargantuan' and 'heaves with fat', with Gold further asserting that the provision of exercise-wear for women of that size was nothing less than the, nowadays unpardonable, crime of normalising obesity. Some months later Gold wrote about the venomous Twitter backlash the article had attracted, detailing some of the vicious, misogynistic comments which had been directed towards her – many from women insulted by her comments on body shape. More unexpectedly though, she also wrote about coming to the realisation that some of her own crueller remarks had been written out of her sense of self-hatred, prompted by her own problem with weight, and sugar addiction. It's an interesting example of how successfully the cycles of policing and self-policing have been bred into women's social DNA, hampering our ability to recognise and resist the objectification in continual operation around us.

THAT'S ME IN THE CORNER

It would be comforting to think that the moment a woman ceases to be seen as flesh and begins to be treated as meat is unmistakable, at least to her. Theoretically, that would then make it more readily resistible. But this is not always the case. In fact, it is more often not the case because, while objectification takes place in the eye of the beholder rather than in the mind of the beheld, this is complicated by the convoluted processes through which the beheld are actively encouraged to view themselves from a similar remove. Feminist philosopher and gender studies academic Sandra Lee Bartky describes this in *Femininity and Domination: Studies in the Phenomenology of Oppression*: 'In the regime of institutionalised heterosexuality woman must make herself "object and prey" for the man ... Woman lives her body as seen by another, by an anonymous patriarchal Other.'

We see what we are seen as, and therefore internalise the gravity of fulfilling what is required of us to fit the picture well. This has implications for women's sexuality too. In *Sex, Politics and Society: The Regulation of Sexuality Since 1800*, the sociologist Jeffrey Weeks points to how the modern version of this problem began to take shape in the backlash to women's changing domestic roles after the end of the Second World War:

> The major legislative reforms of the late 1960's and '70's did little to fundamentally undermine the complex structure of female subordination and the contradictions at the heart of femininity were, in turn, to give rise to a more militant women's movement by the turn of the decade. Female sexuality lay at the centre of these contradictions. Women were necessarily wooed by the great consumer industries but chiefly at first in their roles as controllers of the household purse. Their sexuality could be utilised, stimulated, reshaped as an adjunct to the demands of mass marketing, but it was a sexuality designed to capture the man – cosmetics, clothes, personal accoutrements were big business and essential parts of the reconstructed feminine mystique.

Women's struggle with this shape-shifting pressure to inhabit the 'right' brand of femininity has proved something of a paralytic ever since, with the 'right' brand being carefully reinvented for each new generation. From the hippy ideal of 'free love' prohibiting women use of the word 'no' to the more recent manoeuvring of extreme, formerly niche, BDSM practices into the sexual mainstream, no woman, with the possible exception of a cloistered nun, can escape the knowledge that it is only by circumscribing her own freedoms, and adapting her choices to conform to the patricentric culture and institutions which enclose her, that she can gain approval. To this end, she is the one who must assume full responsibility for making mincemeat of herself.

She can also expect to be continually marketed the idea that the rewards for becoming not only meat but precisely the right kind of meat are boundless. Conversely, those women who cannot be tempted onto the butcher's slab, who are not motivated enough to meet the criteria, or even those who long to stretch out upon it but cannot starve or feminise themselves enough into sufficiently stereotype-aligning representations of womanhood to make the grade, will still not find themselves treated as flesh. They will instead just be stamped the wrong kind of meat which, on principle, can never be rewarded.

Here be the lesbians in comfortable shoes, the overweight, the old-ish, the busy, the indifferent and the already content. These women – and there are a lot of us – will be persistently reminded of the undesirability of their brand of meatiness, and of just how little the pleasure of going through life without bothering to contort oneself into a more readily acceptable version of femininity makes up for that unpleasant fact. It's an effective deterrent, particularly among the young, playing as it does on the insecurities and the restrictions placed on rebellion and self-assertion that Western culture inculcates most women with obedience to from early on in life.

'SAM, 16, QUITS A LEVELS FOR OOH LEVELS!'

The idea of this 'training' was much on my mind a few years ago when I still had to push my daughter in a buggy to the local supermarket. I was painfully aware that whenever we entered, the very first thing her two-year-old eyes would alight on were the rows of tabloid newspapers which someone had taken to leaving spread open at whichever page had the largest, most sexually provocative photo of a semi-naked woman the paper contained. I would never have exposed her to such images but there she was being exposed, nonetheless. It is impossible to explain the meaning of pictures like that to a toddler and it is completely enraging that women still have to.

But what about women who willingly embrace acting as objects? What about glamour modelling, say? Given the average age of the women who pursue it, youth or naivety may sometimes explain their participation, but it's not an accurate enough explanation to entirely dispose of their awkward presence. After all, that idea just plays along with the patriarchy's get-out-of-jail-free card which assumes that young women require paternalistic interventions to protect them from a big bad world they cannot possibly understand.

The trajectory of ye olden time glamour model, pop singer, songwriter and all-round celebrity Samantha Fox is a case in point. Fox first appeared topless on the front cover of the *Sunday People* at the age of sixteen. A lucrative contract with the *Sun* followed and Fox soon became the most famous 'Page 3 Girl' of the 1980s, winning 'Page 3 Girl of the Year' for three years in a row. Deciding to leave topless modelling on a high, Fox retired at the ripe old age of twenty and went on to establish a successful music career. In recent years, she has stated on several different occasions that she has no regrets about her former career and that, because she only worked with photographers whose reputations for professional behaviour on set were impeccable, she was never pressured to perform outside of her comfort zone or subjected to the type of sexual harassment which seems to be synonymous with contemporary glamour modelling. Fox has also been forthright about how glamour modelling enabled her to escape the kind of life that the grim social conditions of her childhood might otherwise have condemned her to. In short, topless modelling gave Fox a shortcut to the kind of lifestyle and opportunities she would otherwise have struggled to access, and she was clearly no simple dupe of cynical forces, as we might like to imagine. Might abusive exploitation at the hands of unscrupulous male photographers be more palatable to us, and more readily understandable, than the notion of some young women's enthusiastic engagement in their own public pornification?

It also has to be said that Fox's story of having to put her songwriting credit on the 'girl band' All Saints song 'Dreams' under her mother's name rather than her own, because the band didn't wish to be tainted by association with her former employment, leaves something of a sour taste in the mouth. Although the media's insistence on persistently reproducing out-of-context images of women who have appeared naked on film for whatever reason – be they glamour or fashion models or actresses for whom nude scenes formed a perfectly logical constituent of a naturalistic drama – makes the band's reticence understandable, if not admirable. But, even acknowledging this, the fact that Fox's own mother was – by Fox's account – not only supportive of but 'ecstatic' about her daughter being offered a topless contract at the age of sixteen is unignorable. This must surely be because, even if it were not illegal (which it is), it's inconceivable to think of the father of a sixteen-year-old working-class boy, in any era, cheering his son on to get his penis out for the front cover of the *Sunday People*. Teenage boys' and adult men's bodies appearing naked and sexualised in the mainstream press is just not done, not campaigned for and never seen as a mark of gender equality, which men need to fight for the right to attain.

So, as uncomfortably judgemental as it may be to hold the choices of female glamour models up against the light of feminist thought, that very fundamental dichotomy remains. Fox's biology made her a publicly sexualise-able object in a way which would have be unthinkable had she been born male. It was only by accepting a role wholly dependent on performing her body for heterosexual male titillation – as with many women of her social and economic class before and since – that she could gain access to the life-changing opportunities which, otherwise, would probably have been denied her.

Topless modelling sits at the extreme end of female sexual objectification, but the double standard it represents is visible everywhere, from professional dress codes that include high heels and make-up for women, to the 'wellness' industry's propagation of the nauseating belief that women unwilling to conform to traditional stereotypes of beautiful, slim and well-groomed femininity are all suffering from some terrible form of self-hatred.

So, if women are constantly being shown the benefits of being meat, how can they possibly object when they find themselves viewed as such? Why would a woman not only consent but covet every opportunity to propose herself as it? Pragmatically speaking, if objectification is going to happen anyway, why not salvage something from the situation for herself? And what good feminist is in a position to forbid the making of that choice?

'Nothing tastes as good as skinny feels' is the oft-quoted line by the supermodel Kate Moss. Although she has since downplayed the import of the quote, referring to it as merely 'a little jingle', it would be hard to argue that she has not spent her professional life being well rewarded for submitting to the bind of this specific dietary philosophy. In terms of the ever-renewing cycle of a woman's 'good' or 'correct' behaviour winning her favour the template is flawless; you make a sacrifice of what your body needs, and quite frequently enjoys, and the body which results from this renunciation will be held up as an ideal of beauty and feted for it. Of course a four-cheese pizza eaten in your tracksuit bottoms doesn't taste as good as that.

But this particularly intransigent bargain and its double deception are real and often paralysing. Because while the arduously acquired physique is being celebrated and rewarded, the very same body will still be looked at, spoken about and, frequently, treated in ways its possessor will find difficult, but over which they will have no control. Even Kate Moss's willingness to be 'on message' about the being skinny business has garnered her more slaps than pats over the years and, like every other highly visible woman, she is constantly subjected to critical, physical and decidedly sexualised scrutiny in the press and online. Should the women who find themselves on the sharp end of this situation raise an objection, however, they will assuredly be told – and here's the ingenuity of the 'controllers of opinion' functioning at their best – that this is the price they should expect to pay for being beautiful, successful and admired. Bitten at both ends, frequently chewed and then, as the saying goes, spat back out again.

While most women will not experience this on the same grand scale as women in the public eye, the trickledown effect is, as always, hard at work on the internet and across social media. Here trolls feast on images of everyday women, criticising their weight, size, shape, what they wear, where they come from and where they appear to be going, all with as much gusto as they then expend on instructing those same women not to complain about it and/or blaming them for allowing such images to be made, or posted, in the first place. Meat and flesh. One to be eaten, one to be left. One we are and one we are made, whether we willingly engage in the process or not.

RIDING TO SUFFRAGE

Still, even the lead boots of women's history move forward, women move them, and eventually everything must change. It helps that boundaries are by their very nature troublesome and permeable. As academic and feminist film critic Christine Gledhill writes:

> Boundaries serve not only to sepa-rate and contain but also to constitute meeting points, instituting contact between spheres the dominant culture seeks to divide. Definition through dif-ferentiation brings new terrain into view. Desire is generated at the boundaries,

stimulating border crossings as well as provoking cultural anxieties.

This must surely be the place where women like Samantha Fox, say, have taken their objectification and activated it for their own benefit. Attempts to repurpose the tools of subjugation have not been without controversy within the feminist movement, and among women more generally, from concerns about the hyper-sexualisation of young girls to the lingering suspicion that we have somehow been conned into becoming the instruments of our own oppression.

It is hardly surprising then that, dealing so explicitly with the always problematic area of the body, the world of exercise and physical fitness has also proven a flashpoint. Women utilising exercise as a means of emancipation from the social restrictions placed on their bodies, as well as the confinements of both their clothes and homes, has a long and illustrious history. In the 1890s the American suffragists and social reformers Susan B. Anthony and Elizabeth Cady Stanton were widely reported in the press as having announced 'woman is riding to suffrage on the bicycle'.

This became increasingly significant as the surge in popularity of cycling among women did much to promote a resurgence in bloomer-wearing. The iconic bloomer – a loosely divided trouser – had first become fashionable in the US in the 1850s and was widely adopted as a healthier, more hygienic and liberating mode of attire. As such, it soon became identified with the women's reform movement. However, it wasn't long before the novelty of women wearing these, hitherto unimaginably revealing, garments was drawing crowds to suffragist rallies all by itself and bloomer wearers came under considerable pressure from within the movement to abandon them as an unwarranted distraction to the greater cause. But the arrival of the bicycle necessitated a practical change to women's dress which more than justified forsaking the heavy, organ-displacing corsetry and obstructively long dresses they had previously been immured within. And so the bloomer returned, triumphant!

Similarly, complicated attitudes greeted the rise of the aerobics craze that swept the US in the 1970s and 80s. While steering clear of a specifically feminist narrative, both Jane Fonda and Judi Sheppard Missett (founder of Jazzercise) were keen to ally their programmes to a more generalised movement towards women's sense of self-empowerment. Until that point, the pursuit of physical fitness had been the preserve of the male population, sited deep within their female-unfriendly gyms. Keen to combat the unflattering – disgust-inducing? – misconception that proper women should not enjoy vigorous exercise, Missett's Jazzercise studios were alone at that time in providing crèche facilities which allowed women with children to come and work out unhindered, as well as salvage a little time out of their days for themselves. Founding her programme initially to fund the Campaign for Economic Democracy, Fonda went on to build a multimillion-dollar empire comprising studio courses, best-selling books and, with the arrival of the home video, wildly successful exercise tapes.

This combination permitted women unprecedented access to the world of exercise and fitness, with all the attendant physical and psychological benefits. Critics, however, pointed out that both Missett's and Fonda's programmes failed to challenge the cultural 'norms' that pressured women into conforming to male fantasies about how their bodies should ideally appear. Some went further and claimed they were cynically promoting oppressive stereotypes of physical beauty for their own financial gain, at a time when feminists were urging women to reject these stereotypes and make their existence as physical beings beholden only to their own bodies' needs. While such arguments were largely ignored by the millions of women who bought into 'The Jane', debates about the multilayered meanings of female physical fitness, and whose purpose it best serves, rumble on.

HERE'S ME AND WHO'S LIKE ME?

More recently, the 'Body Positivity' and 'Body Neutrality' movements have taken up the fight for more explicit acceptance and celebration of those bodies which have traditionally been ignored, sidelined or made into objects of disgust. Obviously, this is a wide-ranging territory of exclusion covering almost anyone who doesn't conform to traditional 'thin white woman' standards of beauty. Indeed, if Serena Williams, who has spent the last twenty years establishing and maintaining her position as one of the greatest tennis players, and athletes, of all time, is still subjected to body-shaming comments, what possible chance can ordinary women have of effecting radical change? For once, however, social media has been on women's side, with groups on Facebook and Tumblr, as well as Instagrammers, forming net-works of support for the propagation and dissemination of images and new attitudes towards black bodies, big bodies, disabled bodies and combinations of all of the above.

In a May 2020 article in *Vogue* fat-accept-ance blogger Stephanie Yeboah wrote:

> As a darker-skinned, black, plus-size woman living in western society, I'd grown up seeing bodies like mine marginalised, insulted, fetishised and demonised. My body – and body shapes similar to mine – had never been in fashion. I grew up being told via the media and the entertainment industry that to be white and thin was to be 'in'. It was beautiful. And anything that didn't meet that standard was considered 'less than'.

Whether these movements can succeed in making the profound, irreversible change that so many women desperately need has yet to be seen. Further on in her article Yeboah sounds a note of caution about a reversion already occurring in these movements which seeks to return focus to white or light-skinned women, or women with big bodies but the tiny waists that hark back to impossible ideals; while in October 2020, the *Guardian* also ran an article, by the body-positive activist and writer Lacey-Jade Christie, drawing attention to the Instagram algorithm's censorship of images of bigger-bodied women. As always, the threat of commodification lurks, with multiple brands already seeking to capitalise on the perceived popularity of the shift in public opinion.

BIRD ON A POLE

As always, few women live in the black and white. So, if we take porn as one extreme – women's bodies existing purely for the gratification of others – and as the other, the women's fitness movement – women taking full control of their bodies – the craze for pole-dancing exercise classes which took off in the 2000s is an interesting point of intersection. For one school of thought, the idea of scantily clad women sliding up and down a pole could only ever evoke images of dingy 70s and 80s strip clubs or the sleaze-in-class-clothing 'gentlemen's clubs' set up later to allow those men the same ogling privileges while reimagining themselves as connoisseurs of the female form rather than merely self-indulgent voyeurs.

Somewhat inevitably, given the strong association of pole dancing with the sex industry, its appearance as a fitness trend quickly gained attention. At the same time, its ambiguous history ensured it could never be viewed as an entirely uncomplicated activity. While doing a little research on this, I came across a number of advertisements for classes and courses, many of which described pole dancing as a 'sport' or an 'art' and, most frequently, as a means of attaining greater fitness, increased strength and flexibility, as well as improving personal confidence. 'Super fun and challenging!' 'Everyone is really friendly in this class!' exclaim the client testimonials on one site, seemingly keen to emphasise the non-sexual narrative – although the word 'sensual' eventually does make an appearance in its copy. Some sites make no reference to pole dancing's less salubrious past, while remaining at pains to tip a jauntily angled hat to the inalienable 'sexiness' of the discipline. Some are more upfront, eager to draw attention to pole dancing's 'erotic' possibilities. What all have in common are the multiple photos of their young, trim, almost entirely female, clientele wearing bikinis or short shorts – which, on balance, seems to be a necessity, given all the thigh-gripping on display – as they hang at unlikely angles from the pole itself. So, while all of that is reasonable enough, I couldn't help noticing how pole-dancing classes really don't bother to gear themselves towards netting male fitness fans. To be honest, I struggle to think of any form of exercise which either derives from such explicitly sexual origins or hawks its 'sexuality unleashing' potential to men at all. But anyway ... as I clicked around the various ads, I happened upon a short film, entitled *Why I Dance*, made in 2015 by US writer/film-maker Melanie Zoey Weinstein. It's about eight minutes long and performed in an airy, well-lit loft studio to the backing track of the gospel song 'Down in the River to Pray'. Each of the sixteen women performers are dressed in black, bondage-style leotards with rips and straps, etc., but subvert the stereotype of heavy 'glamour' make-up with their faces only lightly made up and hair styled naturalistically. The camera follows as they gyrate on the floor and creep over to the pole with all the usual rotating hips, hair flicking, stroking, etc. Individually, they perform routines which include the requisite amounts of spins, deep back bends, hanging upside down by the thighs and spread-eagling. Rather than sporting, or gymnastic, the overall tone is distinctly sexual with lots of porny 'come hither' eye contact with the camera. After the finale, in which the women create various 'sexy' group tableaux, static and otherwise, they fall back into a kind of 'buddy' mode in which they shed their 'sexy' personas, laugh with mild embarrassment and embrace each other in a manner implying an 'I know that you know that I know' post-feminist acknowledgement that the stereotypical sexual roles they have just inhabited, or displayed, were purely performative, offered only to the camera and for the benefit of an unknown audience, rather than for each other. More intriguing, however, is that intercut with all of this are frames of each woman holding a handwritten sign bearing, presumably personal, statements about themselves – 'Raw Vegan Chef', 'Free Spirit', 'Writer', 'Amazon', 'Little Sister', etc. After this there is a further round of signs describing pole dancing's meaning/significance to them: 'Because the expression of my sexuality does not negate my: integrity, intelligence, or autonomy',

'Because my body is mine', 'Because it frees my inner power', 'Because it healed what they tried to break.' The film finishes on a shot of a clothed female crew member holding a sign inscribed with 'To Empower Everyone'. These statements, along with the setting for the performance, emphasise the film-maker's desire to underline a message of female empowerment and the importance of personal choice with regard to sexual self-expression. It is also at pains to portray sexual self-expression as occurring within a mutually supportive female environment, far from the requirement to satisfy the male gaze with which pole dancing is more usually associated. However, that this message is played unquestioningly alongside so many traditional pornographic tropes of hetero-normative male sexual fantasy makes for unsettling viewing, provoked, surely, by the question the film poses about the nature and exercise of women's sexual agency but then fails to engage with: If we are truly doing this for ourselves, why doesn't it look like that? Why, despite the discreet make-up, enviable hair, the bright, healthy, supportive surroundings and the slogans of self-assertion, does this film still look like sixteen grown women desperately trying to give a man a hard-on? If even one woman had cracked a joke in the middle of all the crotch thrusting, I might have been able to buy into the noble premise a little more, but no one was laughing until the serious business of performative sexiness had been completed. Am I being unfair? Should I accept their, obviously, benign intentions at face value? Or is my irritation indicative of a wider question that contemporary women are grappling with?

DOUBLE STAGNATION

If all women are born into a highly sexualised, objectifying culture, which is necessarily hostile to the advancement of their liberties and equality, and this culture becomes the filter through which they experience every aspect of their lives, for the whole of their lives, is it truly possible for them to avoid internalising every single warped reflection with which they are surrounded? And how can they ever be sure? By embracing a sexuality inescapably coloured by the confines of the culture in which we live, can we honestly claim to be the sole arbiters of that sexuality? Or, by rejecting outright all expressions of 'traditional' femininity and sexuality – along with the motives of women who choose to conform to them – do we risk depriving ourselves of the evolving possibilities of sexuality and fall into the trap of taking on the patriarchal policing of the choices other women make about their own bodies?

Does this, in turn, mean that the critical, non-sexual female gaze, or the fear of falling foul of it, is as troublesome to women's freedom of choice, and sexual expression, as the male gaze has always been? If we do indeed, as Sandra Lee Bartky suggests, make 'object and prey' of ourselves, is the logical extension then that we also make 'object and prey' of other women? The continuous recycling of concepts like 'Mean girls', 'Back-stabbing bitches', 'Yummy Mummy versus Slummy Mummy', etc., suggests so. The dif-ficulty of identifying the line which divides carefully considered critique from the knee-jerk impulse to patrol opinions or behaviour which don't readily lend themselves to one's own, necessarily subjective, set of beliefs is only further complicated by the Escher-like inescapabilty of the patriarchal framework in which we live.

One factor surely contributing to this muddying of the waters is the lingering sus-picion that women have been sold a pup by the market forces which encourage them to liberate themselves through continuous acts of consumerism. Show how you embrace and display your sense of agency, individu-ality and sexuality by buying this phone cover, these heels, this incredibly expen-sive handbag/car/surgery, etc. This is what the tag line reads but the true underlying message of 'You must have' is 'You must be' – not *having* xyz may be forgivable, but not *being* xyz is a different matter entirely.

As a consumer we are promised the opportunity to buy our way back 'into place', as long as the place we are striving for goes hand in hand with, to repeat Jeffrey Weeks's phrase, 'the reconstructed feminine mystique'. Somehow, buying an excellent set of power tools and a top-of-the-range ride-along mower don't count towards liberating the 'real' woman within, no matter how practically liberating they might be.

Increasingly intimate demonstrations of a willingness to apply oneself to the task are now expected. So, where once this revolved around selecting the right type of cosmetics and clothes, nowadays displays of an enthusiastic, avaricious sexuality are considered de rigueur. To fulfil this remit with any possibility of success though, we are required to maintain, or at least strive to attain, a fashion-model and porn-actress standard of personal grooming. Once upon a time preserving the perfect weight was sufficient in this area; the flat stomach soon followed; later female pubic hair was added to the list of unacceptably disgusting 'out of place' aspects of women's bodies that had to go. Nowadays, it's pretty much everything from cracked heels and unmanicured fingernails, to the quest for the holy thigh gap, eyebrows groomed into immaculate reproductions of ungroomed eyebrows, and skin which requires so much intervention to look 'natural' that it hardly leaves any time over to advertise it on Instagram as 'without filters'.

Consumerism too has urged the popularisation of BDSM with its accompanying outfits and props – now for sale at all reputable high street sex shops. And while the line is rigorously reinforced that these practices are mostly harmless, the increased expectation placed on young women to be au fait with the mechanics of being bound, beaten and strangled for fun, as well as to possess a willingness to partake in such activities on demand, has a darker side. Anecdotal stories abound of young women wondering if being choked by their partners during sex is unusual and the rising tide of women being killed by their partners during 'rough' sex would seem to bear the terrible reality of this out. Indeed so many men have claimed what is now known as 'The 50 Shades Defence' – alleging the woman in question consented to engage in a sadomasochistic sex act which then 'went wrong', meaning her partner should not be charged with murder because 'she wanted it' – that, in December 2018, the MP Harriet Harman called for a review into the sentencing of one such murderer, declaring: 'No man will ever be accused of murder again if he can always say, "yes she's injured, she wanted it". She will never be able to say, "no I didn't", because he's killed her and therefore she hasn't got a voice.'

The cruel irony at the centre of this is that where once, in the West, the male-centric sexual marketplace insisted a woman's virginity and general ignorance with regard to sexual matters was the greatest indicator of her market value, now it has decided that any reticence or admission of sexual naivety, or insecurity, will immediately cause her stock to plummet.

All the while women are constantly assured that the many purchases that this performance necessitates are, in fact, an emblem of our personal empowerment and the extent of our liberation from ye sex-shaming olden days that our mothers and grandmothers laboured under – the new and exciting means of sex shaming to which we ourselves will likely be subjected are, of course, kept back as a surprise for later on.

And of course, while all of this practice and paraphernalia only adds to the sexual bankability of young women, similar revelations of an avid, experienced sexuality in middle-aged women, and above, is considered wholly unappetising. Expressions of overt sexuality in women over the age of forty-five seem to evoke such negative reactions that the best they can hope for is for their sexuality to be framed as sweet and harmless – and this only in the context of an 'age-appropriate' relationship. Next level down is 'funny', and film and TV shows are strewn with hilarious portrayals of the ridiculous, sexually rapacious older woman; bawdy, available to all and any takers, and eternally oblivious to the fact she is a figure of fun. Worst, however, is the disgust reserved exclusively for older women's bodies operating in a sexual context and driven by desire. Is this due to our inability to separate sexuality from fecundity? Or is it to do with more ancient anxieties about the potential ungovernability of older women who, having slipped the enslavement of their reproductive systems, can no longer be controlled via their fertility and are now free to embrace sex for sex's sake in a manner hitherto available only to men? Perhaps. The visceral negativity provoked by expressions of sexuality in older women, so rarely mirrored in attitudes towards older men, certainly suggest more is at stake than mere cosmetic aversion to ageing bodies.

The irony is that at the same time as older women and women with disabilities are being busily lowered into a well of disgust for their imperfection, the 'perfect' young women themselves, while being constantly pushed towards and praised for their seemingly empowered acts of sexual liberation and sexual self-expression, are also being told that they are vulnerable, confused, incapable of informed choice and in need of paternalistic protection by the male guardians of our culture – young women don't know what they're thinking – but by feminists too – young women don't know what they're doing. This goes hand in glove with the convoluted attitude towards young women and self-objectification, and I can't declare myself immune to this type of thinking either.

I admired the singer Miley Cyrus's sticking up of two fingers to the cynical TV executives who sought to neutralise her emerging adulthood and sexuality with an enforced performance of continuing sexless, unthreatening girlhood. And then, once she had wrenched herself from their clutches, I wished she'd put some clothes on and stop writhing about onstage like the living embodiment of every male music exec's wet dream. My feelings on watching *Why I Dance* is another example because, while sincerely wanting women to be free to do whatever the hell they want with their own bodies – and why else would I be writing this essay? – I was still aware of how cynical I felt about the slotting of slogans about female empowerment into a film which unquestioningly fulfilled every stereotypical, male sexual expectation of women performing on a pole.

So, a difficulty arises because if both of these examples are truthful representations of my thoughts, and both elements within both examples are true for me simultaneously, how do I ever dare hold an opinion at all? If I come down in favour of one side of the argument, I am obliged to refuse identification with the other. However, if I am unwilling to go along with only black-and-white possibilities for truth, then the contradictions I inevitably face seem to lead to an instantaneous paralysis, a halting of all forward motion. I will be trapped and, indeed, I often feel that I am trapped. But I am not alone. This very dilemma is tackled by the media and psychology academics Adrienne Evans and Sarah Riley, in their book *Technologies of Sexiness: Sex, Identity, and Consumer Culture*:

'double stagnation' – sticking points, for example, between a feminist desire to both give voice to women's experience and to challenge what seem to be new forms of oppression dressed up in the wolf's clothing of 'empowerment'.

In analysing this social landscape, feminist theorists have to engage with the complex and contradictory nature of the discourses around contemporary active female sexuality – for example, that it can be experienced as pleasurable and liberating, and yet reproduces an image that appears objectifying.

The concern around whether the experience of empowerment can actually be described in feminist terms *as* empowerment underlies the stuck place between a position of accepting women's accounts, and thereby assuming agency, and seemingly jettisoning feminist aims for female emancipation.

The lack of real momentum in feminism in the supposedly 'post-feminist' period seems to relate, at least in part, to the problem of 'double stagnation'. After all, women, technically, had equal rights and access to opportunities as men. And if women of colour, working-class women, immigrant women, disabled women, single mothers, women living on benefits or below the poverty line, didn't have much of a voice, well, that was to be regretted but ignored as a series of inconvenient truths which could probably be remedied anyway with the exertion of a bit more effort/self-control/compromise/good manners/asking nicely, on the part of the women concerned, right?

And as middle-class white women were being continually assured that, whatever it felt like, true empowerment certainly looked like the ability to deliver a pithy one-liner in a pair of Manolo Blahniks, why on earth would any of them want to resemble those angry, pushy feminists who make life so awkward for everyone else? It was a pretty tiresome time ... when it wasn't just endlessly infuriating. Then, somewhat cata-clysmically, the #MeToo movement arrived and ripped right through the apparent stasis, encouraging women from all backgrounds to work themselves free of the coercive silence, and retributive threats, which so often accompany sexual harassment, abuse and rape, particularly when perpetrated in the workplace. Without doubt #MeToo has been a huge step forward but only a step nonetheless, and it has left many issues, including that of 'double stagnation', in place.

DOUBLE SUCK IT UP!

Of course, the idea of the double is practically woven into the definition of womanhood. The 'damned if you do and damned if you don't' style of rhetoric, which seeks to invigilate our every move, desire and decision, is nothing new and each woman surely has a different example to share. I doubt I am alone in recalling the 'only sluts do "it" but virgins are frigid' mantra of my own adolescence. We know women have to work harder than men to acquire top jobs but then receive far less recognition, and financial renumeration, for their achievements within them. It's still too common for women working outside of the home to feel, and be treated as, fundamentally neglectful of their children, while women who stay at home are deemed to provide terrible role models for their daughters. Try as hard as you can to be as thin as possible, goes the directive, but always hide the true costs of staying that way. Make the most of yourself but don't wear too much make-up. Be sure to stay young, don't look like you're trying to stay young. Women are obsessed with getting pregnant – women who don't want children aren't proper women, etc., etc. So, with all of this already hanging around our necks, do we really want to be on the lookout for more Catch-22s? And even more so in a world which increasingly prioritises the security of inflexible binaries over the frustrations and inconsistencies inherent to meaningful engagement with complex issues? Probably not, but we should because 'double stagnation' is different to these. This double is not imposed from without but self-generates within, and the opposing sides of its conflicts can indeed both be true, concurrently. Confused? I'll go first:

I have no moral problem with the existence of porn but I have a big moral problem with much of the porn that exists. I know that taking care of one's own children is work. I don't think that taking care of your children is the same as work. I think women should wear whatever they like. I cringe when I see women wearing 'Porn Star' T-shirts. I really don't think it's my business to be making these judgements but I also make these judgements and I am reasonably confident that most women, at some point in their lives, struggle with the implications of these and many other double stagnations. But if acknowledging the validity of seemingly contradictory positions occurs so frequently, why is it so paralysing? Surely an old-fashioned list of pros and cons should quickly resolve it? And yet it doesn't and I wonder if this relates back to traditional 'masculine' ideas about what constitutes strength and weakness? Assessing situations quickly, choosing sides and then sticking to them, no matter what, has always been promoted as an enviable sign of character – it doesn't hurt that this also happens to be the definition of the alpha male.

Conversely, history has done all in its power to breed the same simplistic certainty,

confident entitlement and gung-ho deci-
siveness out of women – after all, nothing
throws cold water on the quest for world
domination like the ever-present threat
of violence, rape and murder. With the
enforced constriction of their physical and
intellectual spaces, women, historically, have
often been compelled to approach problem-
solving in less dramatic, more open-ended
ways, whether this has felt intuitive to them
or not. How many women have survived,
and not survived, the effort to rip, roar and
beat bombast and certitude out of them?
How many dread, and have dreaded, arriving at the surrender of Kate's final lines in
The Taming of the Shrew:

My mind hath been as big as one of yours,
My heart as great, my reason haply more,
To bandy word for word and frown for
    frown;
But now I see our lances are but straws,
Our strength as weak, our weakness past
    compare,

That seeming to be most which we indeed
     least are.

What makes it harder is the knowledge
that our culture, indeed the entire global civilisation of which women form nearly 50%,
is mostly founded on societies that have
either historically denigrated or continue
now to denigrate women at the most fundamental level of their humanity, their bodies
– sometimes even before those bodies have
been born – so that what they think and
how they think has been, or is, of no account
whatsoever. And this terrible knowledge
cannot be sidestepped, escaped from or
ignored because that same culture and civilisation, forged by and for men, is women's
culture and civilisation too, the one and only
civilisation of which they can ever be a part.
There may be differing social models, traditions and conventions but there is no other
world. There is no golden time before this
time when it was all different and men and
women gambolled freely together across the

fields of equality. There is no place we can hark back to for aspirational examples of how well things might turn out eventually, or for indications that this ship is turning itself around. There is only what was and now what is. What will be or perhaps, more accurately, what may be is the only hope we possess of radically redefining our culture and civilisation in a way which no longer threatens women's bodies, stifles their ambitions, diminishes their contributions, or disregards their objections.

Surely such a shift isn't impossible, after all I love Shakespeare too and, although it has not always felt like it, I know his works belong to me as much as any man who has ever read them. They are my artistic heritage, my intellectual right, and so their place at the centre of our culture is also my place. The centre of our culture is every woman's place whether she gives a damn about Shakespeare or not. 'Be polite', 'Be nice', 'Be grateful' are the traditional warnings given to women by the gatekeepers of our civilisation, along with the unspoken threat that failure to do so will exclude them from the public discourse and, sometimes, life itself. But from women's repurposing of Trump's dismissal of Hillary Clinton as a 'nasty woman' into a slogan of emancipation, to their widely expressed fury at Health Secretary Matt Hancock's advice to MP Dr Rosena Allin-Khan that she watch her tone, for daring to question his handling of the coronavirus pandemic, women's patience with male commands, and the obligation to operate within frameworks of men's choosing, seems to have run out. And why should the 'double stagnation' not ultimately, and ironically, prove to be a help rather than a hindrance in supporting this change? Where once singularity of purpose and overweening confidence were the Damoclean sword held over women's heads as a symbol of their vacillating inferiority, now, with the world in flames around us, perhaps this very aptitude for grappling with contradiction will prove the way forward? Perhaps

it will enable us to finally cross the boundaries that desperately need to be crossed in
order for governments and communities
alike to tackle the looming climate crisis?
Perhaps the ability to understand the merits
of competing disparities will prove more
effective at building bridges between communities long set at each other's throats by
patriarchal, capitalist systems whose ends
the maintaining of division has served until
now? Perhaps the notable success of women
heads of state in dealing with the coronavirus pandemic suggests there is some truth
in these declarations? Perhaps. I don't think
there's only one answer, and that's the point.

THE TAMER TAMED

So, maybe I should end where I started, with
an acknowledgement that women are not
all the same, are not all trying to get to the
same place and that, perhaps, there is no one
place for all of us to get to together. What
we have in common though is that, at one

time or another, in one way or another, we have all been seen, or treated, as matter out of place in a world we have every right to call our own. We have seen it. Felt it. Lived it. Died it. Had it open chasms inside us. Had it waste our time. The disgust I have been writing about, which has been deployed so successfully in the war against women making and naming our own places in the world, has succeeded in surrounding us and even managed to creep inside of us. We can be sure it will not dissipate by itself and it will not stop being wielded as a weapon until it is no longer effective. The journey to rendering this disgust obsolete begins with women noticing and identifying it for what it is and it will end only when we have taught ourselves, and everyone else, to refuse it at every turn. Only then, as Mary Douglas might say, will the taboos placed upon us fall away and the universe be revised.

December 2020

AFTERWORD

Just as the proofs of this essay were going to the printers, Sarah Everard was kidnapped and murdered in south London. She was only walking home from her friend's house, but because she was a woman, alone in the street after dark, she became number 119 on the list of women murdered by a man in the UK in the previous twelve months. While the hunt for her killer progressed, women were warned to stay indoors. This was their place and the great outdoors at night was not. The awful arbitrariness of Sarah Everard's abduction and killing – and coming after a year of coronavirus restrictions in which women have been doubly restricted by the dangers of being outside after dark – led to an eruption of grief, fury and frustration. Women shared their stories of harassment, abuse and assault. They spoke of their fear and anxiety as well as their utter exhaustion at having to live in a constant state of hyper-vigilance. Who habitually walks home in the dark with their keys between their fingers, looking over their shoulders and always ready to run? they asked. The universal reply was, who hasn't? Why, they asked, must one half of the population live without the basic freedom of movement afforded so unques-tioningly to the other? And why is violence towards women seen as a problem for women alone to solve when women are not the perpetrators? Then a Metropolitan police officer, Wayne Couzens, was charged with Sarah Everard's kidnap and murder, and the police force themselves decided that the best way to deal with breaches of coronavirus restrictions at a vigil held in Sarah Everard's memory on Clapham Common, near the site she was last seen alive, was to break it up, violently. This led to shameful scenes of women being thrown to the ground, cuffed and dragged away from a peaceful act of public mourning. It stood in stark contrast to the discretion and solidarity adopted during the policing of the previous summer's, equally restriction-breaking, Black Lives Matter protests. Might this be because racism is perceived to be a volatile political issue, with deep institutional roots and the potential to cause major social disruption, while misogyny never is? I think so. After all, misogyny has always been the most socially acceptable hatred, relegated to the domestic and private realm and, more often than not, just seen as a bit of a joke. Men who murder out of it are not viewed as representatives of a deep-seated, institutional blindness to the essential humanity, rights of and well-being of women. They are excused and explained away as weirdos and anomalies. Their hatred of women, their desire to do harm to their bodies, either physically or sexually, is simply not taken seriously. It's not even seen as hatred and, most often, it is considered to have been provoked in the first place. And, let's face it, when a crowd of grieving women don't do what they're told, it's pretty easy to throw them to the ground, physically restrain them and cart them away. I mean, that's how it's always been, hasn't it? Do what you're told, or I'll give you a smack. So, if even the police do not recognise women's right to protest the threat of violence and harassment under which they continually live, then who does? Who will?

In the weeks after Sarah Everard's murder, the World Health Organisation published a report stating that one in three women globally experience physical or sexual violence during their lifetimes. That's about 736 million women's bodies that have been subjected to violence. That is 736 million women's lives that have been forever changed by violence and by a violence that can be inflicted upon them solely because they are women. We didn't start a war, but a war is being waged on us, nonetheless. Staying indoors is not the answer – most of it happens in there anyway. The outdoor life isn't for us either it seems – not according to the police – while in the media, online, everywhere we can be seen and heard, we are just inviting our own abuse and silencing, apparently. The willingness to passively accept this as the status quo for women is a stain on contemporary society and an affront to human dignity.

So then, to all those who have never been bothered to seriously think about the cancerous implications of misogyny for women, either individually or collectively, or for our society as a whole, I have a question. Two questions. The first is: if you, as a person of flesh and blood, thought and feeling, who doesn't want to be murdered or raped, who doesn't want to be hurt or humiliated, or live in the constant fear of it simply for inhabiting the body you do, who doesn't want to have to rear your daughters into the expectation of eventually joining this endless malevolent cycle or your sons to feel eternally implicated in its perpetuation, in short if you were us, women, what would you do? And what are you going to do now?

March 2021

ACKNOWLEDGEMENTS

Thank you to Helen Conford for her thoughtful editing. Thank you to Anakana Schofield for her invaluable support. Thank you to Wellcome Collection for inviting me into their wonders. And thank you to William and Éadaoin most of all.

wellcome collection

Wellcome Collection books explore health and human experience. From birth and beginnings to illness and loss, our books grapple with life's big questions through compelling writing and beautiful design. We work in partnership with leading independent publisher Profile Books.

Wellcome Collection is a free museum that aims to challenge how we all think and feel about health by connecting science, medicine, life and art. It is part of Wellcome, a global charitable foundation that supports science to solve urgent health challenges, working in more than seventy countries, with a focus on mental health, global heating and infectious diseases.

wellcomecollection.org